The Kindness of Strangers

EDITED BY
DON GEORGE

LONELY PLANET PUBLICATIONS
Melbourne • Oakland • London • Paris

The Kindness of Strangers

Published by Lonely Planet Publications

Head Office:
90 Maribyrnong Street, Footscray, Vic 3011, Australia
Locked Bag 1, Footscray, Vic 3011, Australia

Branches:
150 Linden Street, Oakland CA 94607, USA
10a Spring Place, London NW5 3BH, UK
1 rue Dahomey, 75011, Paris, France

Published 2003
Printed by The Bookmaker International Ltd
Printed in China
0001 UK

Edited by Meaghan Amor
Designed by Daniel New

National Library of Australia Cataloguing-in-Publication entry

The Kindness of Strangers

ISBN 1 74059 590 4.

1. Voyages and travels. 2. Travel writing. I. George,
Donald W.

910.4

© Lonely Planet and contributors 2003.

Contents

THE DALAI LAMA

Preface

IF WE REALLY THINK about it, our very survival, even today, depends upon the acts and kindness of so many people. Right from the moment of our birth, we are under the care and kindness of our parents; later in life, when facing the sufferings of disease and old age, we are again dependent on the kindness of others. If at the beginning and end of our lives we depend upon others' kindness, why then in the middle should we not act kindly towards others?

Anyone who considers himself or herself, above all, a member of the human family should develop a kind heart. It is a powerful feeling that we should consciously develop and apply. Instead we often neglect it, particularly in our prime years when we experience a false sense of security.

Kindness and compassion are among the principal values that make our lives meaningful. They are a source of lasting happiness and joy. They are the foundation of a good heart, the heart of one who acts out of a desire to help others.

Through kindness, through affection, through honesty, through truth and justice towards all others, we benefit ourselves as well. This is a matter of common sense. There is no denying that consideration of others is worthwhile. Our own happiness is inextricably bound up with the happiness of others. Similarly, if society suffers, we ourselves suffer. Nor is there any denying that the more our hearts and minds are afflicted with ill will, the more miserable we become.

I believe that we are all to some extent moved by an inability to bear the sight of another's suffering. It is this that, when we see someone in trouble, stirs some feeling in us to go and see if there is anything we can do to help. Moreover, I believe that alongside our natural ability to empathise with others, we also have a need for others' kindness, which runs like a thread throughout our whole life.

At any given moment there must be hundreds of millions of acts of kindness taking place around the world. Although there will undoubtedly be many acts of violence in progress at the same time, these will surely be far fewer. Perhaps this kind of good news is not remarked upon precisely because there is so much of it. Nevertheless, I greatly appreciate the theme of this book that gathers stories of kindness received when it was most needed and perhaps least expected. I am sure they will inspire everyone who reads them, encouraging each of us to take whatever opportunities arise to be kind to others in turn. And in so doing we will contribute actively to creating a more peaceful, harmonious and friendly world.

HIS HOLINESS THE DALAI LAMA

Introduction

IN TWENTY-FIVE YEARS of wandering the world, I have learned two things: the first is that when you travel, at some point you will find yourself in a dire predicament – out of money, out of food, unable to find a hotel room, lost in a big city or on a remote trail, stranded in the middle of nowhere. The second is that someone will miraculously emerge to take care of you – to lend you money, feed you, put you up for the night, lead you to where you want to go. Whatever the situation, dramatic or mundane, some stranger will save you.

The moral of this is simple and clear: human beings care about each other. Whatever their background, religion, culture and condition, on a person-to-person level, just about everyone everywhere wants to be good to others.

This message, which we all know in our hearts, periodically gets beaten down or drowned out by world affairs. Then ignorance, greed and divisiveness take hold. Despair and distrust abound. Stereotypes are sown and spread. Threats are brandished; missiles are primed. Fearful spectres are invoked and dispatched. The global rifts grow.

This book is meant to bridge those rifts, to remind us that we are all members of one grand, globe-encircling family.

The Kindness of Strangers itself is a product of many kindnesses. When I began to compile this book, I asked some of my favourite writers if they had their own examples of kindness on the road.

Everyone did, and many interrupted all-consuming projects to compose pieces. At the same time, Lonely Planet sponsored a competition on its website, inviting readers to send in their tales; we received hundreds more entries than we expected. Encouraged, I dared to dream and wrote to His Holiness the Dalai Lama, asking if he might be willing to write a preface for the book. Over the ensuing months, I and a team of other Lonely Planet editors steeped ourselves in the more than four hundred stories we received – our dispositions growing brighter and brighter as we read – until we narrowed the selection to the twenty-six pieces in this collection. Wonderfully, and fittingly, the resulting book presents world-renowned authors side by side with writers who have never been published before. And as a final blessing, His Holiness the Dalai Lama contributed an eloquent and inspiring preface.

This anthology is a celebration of kindness and of the connections that kindness creates: those unexpected encounters that transfigure and transform us and forge living links with the larger world. For Pico Iyer, this connection comes in the form of a trishaw driver in Mandalay; for Alice Waters, it is a meagre meal with a boy in rural Turkey. It strikes Dave Eggers on a simple stroll along Havana's Malecón, and Tim Cahill when he tracks a rare tiger on the Turkish border with Iraq. For Simon Winchester, kindness is personified in an English vicar and his wife on a remote Atlantic island; for Sarah Levin, it is a bony bicyclist in Tanzania. For Beth Kephart, it appears as a bowl of soup in Seville; for James D. Houston, it's the gift of a coat hanger on Hawaii's Big Island.

Sometimes the kindness connection is fused with humour, as Rolf Potts discovers when he is 'adopted' by a gregarious businessman in Beirut, Douglas Cruickshank learns from a loquacious London cabbie – in whose cab he leaves all his money – and Carolyn Swindell finds when she tries to buy suitable Argentinean underwear.

And sometimes it arrives in a more threatening guise: Nicholas Crane goes to Afghanistan to help the locals, but ends up needing their help to get out alive; Laurie McAndish King and her friend are enjoying the ride to their Tunisian hotel offered by a seemingly generous man they met at a bar, until two locals follow them and run his car off the road; Amanda Jones loses the trail back to camp on a midnight walk in the Sahara, and ends up relying on a Wodaabe tribesman with whom she cannot even speak; Anthony Sattin undertakes a Palestinian pilgrimage and finds himself facing a hostile crowd of rock-toting teenagers; and Jeff Greenwald embarks on a joyride through the US Southwest with an odd couple – who turn out to be much more dangerous than he ever dreamed.

And yet in all these instances, in every story in this book, kindness prevails.

As it has prevailed in all my own wanderings. My travels through the years have been graced by innumerable acts of kindness, great and small: the Greek family who spontaneously shared their Easter celebration with my family; the Japanese truck driver who detoured an hour to deliver me to a village doorstep; the American couple I met on a train who treated me to a five-course feast on our arrival in Vienna; the Kenyan craftsman who handed me an exquisite elephant he had just carved; the young boy in Cairo who appeared like an angel to take me by the hand and lead me out of a sinister neighbourhood. Time after time, I have been the grateful recipient of directions proffered, meals offered, lifts in taxis and trucks and *tuk-tuks*, futons on far-flung floors.

This accumulation has led me to believe that kindness is the planet's key – the impulse of our evolution, the end of our destiny.

The other evening I was buying milk at my local convenience store when I saw an Asian woman puzzling over a map. 'Can I help you?' I asked.

'Do you know where is?' she said in a Chinese accent, holding out a rain-spattered piece of paper with an address scrawled on it. We peered at her map together, until I finally located the almost invisible cul-de-sac. 'That's going to be hard for you to find,' I said. 'Just follow me. I'll take you there.'

Two days later, on a San Francisco cable car, a stout man in a thick sweater and a duffle cap was turning his pockets inside out. 'I've left me wallet in the hotel room,' he told the gripman. Suddenly I was dipping into my own pocket. 'I've got it!' I said and handed over the fare. 'Thank you, sir!' the man said, pumping my arm with a craggy, callused hand.

Before I began editing this book, I don't know if I would have helped these people. But immersing myself in these stories has had a transformative effect: I find myself going out of my way to help people now – and feeling a fresh flush of energy, optimism and goodwill whenever I do. The kindness connection.

I hope this book inspires you in this way, too, for the truth is that kindness is ours to withhold or bestow. If we live every day, whether at home or away, with kindness, if we approach the world with a sense of wonder and curiosity and appreciation, if we encounter others with respect and openness, if we see our human differences as enriching rather than threatening, we will go a long way toward creating a world graced, interlaced, with peace and opportunity.

The Kindness of Strangers began as a simple collection of travellers' tales around a common theme. But as it has come together, it has cohered into something more: a palpable parable of how we are all intricately interconnected on life's journey, every day, everywhere. These richly individual tales all embody the same final truth: we are each other's greatest gift. The kindness of strangers is ours to give and to take; we shape the world with each embrace.

DON GEORGE

The Matter of Kindness

JAN MORRIS

Jan Morris was born in 1926 and has published some forty books of history, travel, autobiography and fiction. She is Welsh and lives in the top left-hand corner of Wales, when she is not travelling the world as she has been doing almost incessantly for half a century. She says her most recent book, *Trieste and the Meaning of Nowhere*, is to be her last, but that doesn't count a retrospective collection of travel pieces and reportage to be published in the USA in 2003, under the grandiloquent title *The World*.

A YEAR OR TWO AGO, on a wet morning, I fell over in the filthily potholed Haymarket in St Petersburg, Russia (which had been Leningrad last time I was there). *What* a mess I was in! My jeans were torn, I was dripping with mud, my books, bag and papers were strewn all over the place, and for the life of me I couldn't get up again. It was no consolation to me to remember that the murderer Raskolnikov, in *Crime and Punishment*, had knelt and kissed the ground almost at the very same spot. I was most certainly not in a kissing mood, as I slithered, scrabbled and cursed impotently in the muck.

A citizen – I nearly said a Comrade – was there to save me. He helped me to my feet. He gathered my scattered possessions. He took me to his shabby neighbouring apartment, and while he brushed down my coat and scrubbed my shoes, allowed me to wash myself in his far from luxurious bathroom. Having found some antiseptic for my grazed knee, he made me coffee and saw me solicitously down to the street. I have never seen him again, but I have come to think of him since as half-mythical.

I suppose most travellers have experienced the kindness of strangers at one time or another, and I am not alone, I am sure, in thinking of it in allegorical terms. Good Samaritans are familiar figures of art and fable. They enter narratives sidelong, out of the mist, or they are glimpsed across empty landscapes, or they arrive melodramatically at a moment of climax, or they snatch unfortunates out of city mud.

And then they disappear. For the point about them is that they *are* strangers. They come, do something helpful and go away. They are the emblematic emissaries of Kindness, with a capital K.

I believe in Kindness. Well, you may retort, who doesn't? But I believe in it rather as religious people believe in God. I think it is the answer to almost all our problems: from the miseries of divorce to nuclear proliferation. If humanity learnt to gauge its every action by the simple criterion of kindness – always to ask if it is, on balance, the *kindest* thing to do? – the world would be much happier. Of course we all know that sometimes it is kind to be cruel, and that none of us can be kind all the time; but still, kindness offers us an uncomplicated morality, liberated from every species of mumbo jumbo, the spells of witch doctors or the theology of professors. After all, wise men as varied as Chekhov and the fourteenth Dalai Lama have claimed that kindness actually *is* their religion!

The most striking manifestation of kindness is certainly the kindness of strangers. We generally expect our friends and relatives to be kind, just as we are not in the least surprised when our sworn enemies are beastly. But when we are befriended in misfortune by people we have never in our lives seen before, then we may see kindness most suggestively displayed, as though these small actions represent the vast, mostly untapped potential of the emotion.

The Kindly Stranger, in my mind, is related to the Righteous Gentile, the generic figure of Jewish tradition who demonstrates that human understanding transcends even the grandest convictions of organised religion. The Righteous Gentile is, by definition, an outsider, or he would be just another Righteous Jew; and the Kindly Stranger is an outsider too, or he would not be a stranger. The most celebrated of all the company was the original Good Samaritan, who came to the rescue of a mugged wayfarer on the road from Jerusalem to Jericho. He was doubly a stranger, so to speak, being himself some kind of heretical half-caste foreigner, and he has been held up for admiration down the centuries for this very reason – that he had nothing in common with the beaten-up traveller across the way, and was probably never going to see him again.

Mind you, I suspect all this is often true of strangers who are kind to us. They feel compelled to help us just because they have nothing to do with us, and are reasonably sure they're never going to set eyes on us again. They are simply sorry for us, and pity can be the most easily satisfied of emotions – the more outlandish and lonely the sufferer is, the easier to satisfy it. Haven't you sometimes walked on in a glow of self-esteem because you have tipped a few bucks to some pitiably unprepossessing and unfashionably ethnic panhandler? Wouldn't you find it harder to respond to a mendicant of your own sort: well dressed, healthy, talking your own language, looking not at all unlike your cousin Julian and asking you for a dollar to buy a cup of tea?

It can be more difficult to be kind to friends, too, than to strangers. Long acquaintance with anybody is by no means always conducive to kindness. Boredom, irritation, insight, disillusion, the broadening of experience, the sharpening of prejudices – all mean that sympathy can be hardest to cherish when you are dealing with the one you know the best, even the one you love the best. By definition the Kindly Stranger must be alien to his beneficiary, but I have a disturbing feeling that the Kindly Friend, the Kindly Neighbour, the Kindly Relative or the Kindly Spouse might be a worthier subject of parable, or for that matter a better hero or heroine for this book.

Never mind, they are the gestures of total strangers that we are celebrating here, and they certainly provide the most elemental illustrations for the whole matter of kindness. You may be moved and inspired by the loyalty of old married couples; you may marvel at the undying patience of mothers towards their handicapped children; stories of comradeship in battle or the changeless devotion of wives to murderers in gaol may bring the tears to your eyes. Kindness is really, so to speak, all of a piece – an absolute, which cannot be graded; but its most symbolical expression is the sudden, unpremeditated act of sympathy, offered without hope of reward to an unknown and perhaps unappealing soul in distress – to a foreigner, a truculent vagrant, an unwashed backpacker or a cat.

Especially, in my own mind, to the cat, because we don't know if a creature of another species even possesses a sense of gratitude. Lions in fables do, but I'm not so sure about thuggish backstreet tomcats; and certainly the greater the gap between the giver and the receiver, the more powerful the symbolism.

When, years ago, I was succoured in a bout of sickness by a Sherpa family in eastern Nepal, it was almost as though I was befriended by aliens. Few Europeans, if any, had ever been to their village in those days, and the smoky house in which I lay flickered mysteriously with butter candles around golden images, while women moved shadowily about, speaking in unknown tongues, and sometimes bringing me victuals from nowhere. The kindness of this family of strangers, though, was utter, and the fact that I didn't even know the local words for 'thank you' made the experience all the more allegorical.

It had a profound effect on me – I can still recapture the exact emotions I felt then, half a century later – and fortunately kindness is catching. Nobody is kind all the time, but in the illimitable order of all things, in my view, every little bit helps. 'Go, and do thou likewise,' Jesus told his interlocutor at the end of the Good Samaritan parable, and perhaps if the charity of a stranger has saved us from ignominy far away, we are likely to be a little less testy ourselves when we emerge ill-tempered from a Himalayan fever, or return home from St Petersburg, some cold and drizzly evening, to find that our beloved has gone away for the weekend without letting us know, and we haven't got a damned door key.

Meeting Maung-Maung

PICO IYER

Pico Iyer is the author of several books about the romance between cultures, including *Video Night in Kathmandu*, *The Lady and the Monk*, *The Global Soul* and a novel, *Abandon*. A short sequel to the story of Maung-Maung that is recorded in these pages, appears in a recent afterword to *Video Night in Kathmandu*. Iyer lives in suburban Japan, encircled by strangeness, kindness and very kind strangers at every turn.

From *Video Night in Kathmandu* by Pico Iyer, copyright © 1988 by Pico Iyer. Used by permission of Alfred A. Knopf, a division of Random House, Inc.

I FIRST MET MAUNG-MAUNG as I stumbled off a sixteen-hour third-class overnight train from Rangoon to Mandalay. He was standing outside the station, waiting to pick up tourists; a scrawny fellow in his late twenties, with a sailor's cap, a beard, a torn white shirt above his *lungi*, and an open, rough-hewn face – a typical tout, in short. Beside him stood his trishaw. On one side was painted the legend 'My Life'; on the other, 'B.Sc. (Maths)'.

We haggled for a few minutes. Then Maung-Maung smilingly persuaded me to part with a somewhat inflated fare – twenty cents – for the trip across town, and together we began cruising through the wide, sunny boulevards of the city of kings. As we set off, we began to exchange the usual questions – age, place of birth, marital status and education – and before long we found that our answers often jibed. Soon, indeed, the conversation was proceeding swimmingly. A little while into our talk, my driver, while carefully steering his trishaw with one hand, sank the other into his pocket and handed back to me a piece of jade. I admired it dutifully, then extended it back in his direction. 'No,' he said. 'This is present.'

Where, I instantly wondered, was the catch – was he framing me, or cunningly putting me in his debt? What was the small print? What did he want?

'I want you,' said Maung-Maung, 'to have something so you can always remember me. Also, so you can always have happy memories of Mandalay.' I did not know how to respond. 'You see,' he went on, 'if I love other people, they will love me. It is like Newton's law, or Archimedes.'

This was not what I had expected. 'I think,' he added, 'it is always good to apply physics to life.'

That I did not doubt. But still I was somewhat taken aback.

'Did you study physics at school?'

'No, I study physics in college. You see, I am graduate from University of Mandalay – B.Sc. Mathematics.' He waved with pride at the inscription on the side of his trishaw.

'And you completed all your studies?'

'Yes. B.Sc. Mathematics.'

'Then why are you working in this kind of job?'

'Other jobs are difficult. You see, here in Burma, a teacher earns only two hundred fifty kyats [US$30] in a month. Managing director has only one thousand kyats [US$125]. Even president makes only four thousand kyats [US$500]. For me, I do not make much money. But in this job, I can meet tourist and improve my English. Experience, I believe, is the best teacher.'

'But surely you could earn much more just by driving a horse cart?'

'I am Buddhist,' Maung-Maung reminded me gently, as he went pedalling calmly through the streets. 'I do not want to inflict harm on any living creature. If I hit horse in this life, in next life I come back as horse.'

'So,' – I was still sceptical – 'you live off tourists instead?'

'Yes,' he said, turning around to give me a smile. My irony, it seems, was wasted. 'Until two years ago, in my village in Shan States, I had never seen a tourist.'

'Never?'

'Only in movies.' Again he smiled back at me.

I was still trying to puzzle out why a university graduate would be content with such a humble job when Maung-Maung, as he pedalled, reached into the basket perched in front of his handle-bars and pulled out a thick leather book. Looking ahead as he steered, he handed it back to me to read. Reluctantly I opened it, bracing myself for porno postcards or other illicit souvenirs. Inside, however, was nothing but a series of black-and-white snapshots. Every one of them had been painstakingly annotated in English: 'My Headmaster', 'My Monk', 'My Brothers and Sisters', 'My Friend's Girlfriend'. And his own girlfriend? 'I had picture before. But after she broke my heart, and fall in love with other people, I tear it out.'

At the very back of his book, in textbook English, Maung-Maung had carefully inscribed the principles by which he lived.

1) Abstain from violence.
2) Abstain from illicit sexual intercourse.
3) Abstain from intoxicants of all kinds.
4) Always be helpful.
5) Always be kind.

'It must be hard,' I said dryly, 'to stick to all these rules.'

'Yes. It is not always easy,' he confessed. 'But I must try. If people ask me for food, my monk tell me, I must always give them money. But if they want money for playing cards, I must give them no help. My monk also explain I must always give forgiveness – even to people who hurt me. If you put air into volleyball and throw it against wall, it bounces back. But if you do not put in air, what happens? It collapses against wall.'

Faith, in short, was its own vindication.

I was now beginning to suspect that I would find no more engaging guide to Mandalay than Maung-Maung, so I asked him if he would agree to show me around. 'Yes, thank you very much. But first, please, I would like you to see my home.'

Ah, I thought, here comes the setup. Once I'm in his house, far from the centre of a city I don't know, he will drop a drug in my tea or pull out a knife or even bring in a few accomplices. I will find out too late that his friendliness is only a means to an end.

Maung-Maung did nothing to dispel these suspicions as he pedalled the trishaw off the main street and we began to pass through dirty alleyways and down narrow lanes of run-down shacks. At last we pulled up before a hut, fronted with weeds. Smiling proudly, he got off and asked me to enter.

There was not much to see inside his tiny room. There was a cot on which sat a young man, his head buried in his hands. There was another cot, on which Maung-Maung invited me to sit as he introduced me to his roommate. The only other piece of furniture was a blackboard in a corner on which my host had written out his lifelong pledge to be of service to tourists: 'All tourist people are my bread and butter. So I need to help everything as I could. If I

21

do not help them, they will never forgive me because I fully understand their love or sincerity. I don't have enough money, but I need to pay their gratitude at one day.'

I sat down, not sure what was meant to happen next. For a few minutes, we made desultory conversation. His home, Maung-Maung explained, cost thirty kyats [US$4] a month. This other man was also a university graduate, but he had no job: every night, he got drunk. Then, after a few moments of reflection, my host reached down to the floor next to his bed and picked up what I took to be his two most valuable belongings.

Solemnly, he handed the first of them to me. It was a sociology textbook from Australia. Its title was *Life in Modern America*. Then, as gently as if it were his Bible, Maung-Maung passed across the other volume, a dusty old English-Burmese dictionary, its yellowed pages falling from their covers. 'Every night,' he explained, 'after I am finished on trishaw, I come here and read this. Also, every word I do not know I look up.' Inside the front cover, he had copied out a few specimen sentences. 'If you do this, you may end up in jail. My heart is lacerated by what you said. What a lark.'

I was touched by his show of trust. But I also felt as uncertain as an actor walking through a play he hasn't read. Perhaps, I said a little uneasily, we should go now, so we can be sure of seeing all the sights of Mandalay before sundown. 'Do not worry,' Maung-Maung assured me with a quiet smile, 'we will see everything. I know how long the trip will take. But first, please, I would like you to see this.'

Reaching under his bed, he pulled out what was clearly his most precious treasure of all. With a mixture of shyness and pride, he handed over a thick black notebook. I looked at the cover for markings and, finding none, opened it up. Inside, placed in alphabetical order, was every single letter he had ever received from a foreign visitor. Every one was meticulously dated and annotated; many were accompanied by handwritten testimonials or reminiscences from the tourists Maung-Maung had met. On some pages, he had affixed wrinkled passport photos of his foreign visitors by which he could remember them.

Toward the end of the book, Maung-Maung had composed a two-page essay, laboriously inscribed in neat and grammatical English, called 'Guide to Jewellery'. It was followed by two further monographs, 'For You' and 'For the Tourists'. In them, Maung-Maung warned visitors against 'twisty characters', explained something of the history and beauty of Mandalay, and told his readers not to trust him until he had proved worthy of their trust.

Made quiet by this labour of love, I looked up. 'This must have taken you a long time to write.'

'Yes,' he replied with a bashful smile. 'I have to look many times at dictionary. But it is my pleasure to help tourists.'

I went back to flipping through the book. At the very end of the volume, carefully copied out, was a final four-page essay, entitled 'My Life'.

He had grown up, Maung-Maung wrote, in a small village, the eldest of ten children. His mother had never learned to read, and feeling that her disability made her 'blind', she was determined that her children go to school. It was not easy, because his father was a farmer and earned only three hundred kyats a month. Still, Maung-Maung, as the eldest, was able to complete his education at the local school.

When he finished, he told his parents that he wanted to go to university. Sorrowfully, they told him that they could not afford it – they had given him all they had for his schooling. He knew that was true, but still he was set on continuing his studies. 'I have hand. I have head. I have legs,' he told them. 'I wish to stand on my own legs.' With that, he left his village and went to Mandalay. Deeply wounded by his desertion, his parents did not speak to him for a year.

In Mandalay, Maung-Maung's narrative continued, he had begun to finance his studies by digging holes – he got four kyats for every hole. Then he got a job cleaning clothes. Then he went to a monastery and washed dishes and clothes in exchange for board and lodging. Finally, he took a night job as a trishaw driver.

When they heard of that, his parents were shocked. 'They think I go with prostitutes. Everyone looks down on trishaw driver. Also other trishaw drivers hate me because I am a student. I do not want to quarrel with them. But I do not like it when they say dirty things or go with prostitutes.' Nevertheless, after graduation Maung-Maung decided to pay seven kyats a day to rent a trishaw full-time. Sometimes, he wrote, he made less than one kyat a day, and many nights he slept in his vehicle in the hope of catching the first tourists of the day. He was a poor man, he went on, but he made more money than his father. Most important, he made many friends. And through riding his trishaw he had begun to learn English.

His dream, Maung-Maung's essay concluded, was to buy his own trishaw. But that cost US$400. And his greatest dream was, one day, to get a 'Further Certificate' in mathematics. He had already planned the details of that far-off moment when he could invite his parents to his graduation. 'I must hire taxi. I must buy English suit. I must pay for my parents to come to Mandalay. I know that it is expensive, but I want to express my gratitude to my parents. They are my lovers.'

When I finished the essay, Maung-Maung smiled back his gratitude, and gave me a tour of the city as he had promised.

Everything Come Round

JAMES D. HOUSTON

James D. Houston is the author of seven novels, most recently *Snow Mountain Passage*, named as one of The Year's Best Books by the *Los Angeles Times* and the *Washington Post*. Among his several nonfiction works are *In the Ring of Fire: A Pacific Basin Journey*, and *Farewell to Manzanar*, co-authored with his wife Jeanne Wakatsuki Houston, the story of her family's experience during and after World War II internment. Formerly a Distinguished Visiting Writer at the University of Hawaii, and the recipient of two American Book Awards, he lives in Santa Cruz, California.

'THE BIG ISLAND is the biggest of them all,' he said, when I called from Honolulu. 'It is the youngest and also the wildest.' With an odd note of glee he added, 'Where we are, you can't even get fire insurance. Trucks literally won't come down here, the roads are so overgrown. So get your butt into Hilo by midafternoon. You don't want to be looking for this place in the dark.'

I'd recently landed a short-term job at the University of Hawaii and had flown in a month before teaching started, giving myself some time to roam around the islands a bit, with no fixed agenda, just to see what I could see. This back-to-the-land friend of mine from Marin County had bought a lot down on the south coast where he was building a house in an impenetrable guava and *hau* tree thicket. He'd put me up, he said, and be my local guide. From there I planned to island-hop back to Oahu by way of Maui and Molokai.

The day before I took off I came across an ad in the Honolulu paper for an apartment that sounded exactly like what I'd need when I returned. The only time the owner could show it to me was perilously close to my flight time, but I agreed to meet him, and that was my first mistake.

His building turned out to be almost as inaccessible as my friend's Big Island hide-out. Inaccessible to me, at any rate, still new to the city's maze of one-way streets and no-turn lanes and roads that circle old volcanic craters. I was late for the appointment, which put me out on the airport freeway during the first crunch of the afternoon commute, which caused me to miss my plane.

Sitting very still in the departure lounge, trying to quell my road rage, I told myself that landing at five o'clock instead of three was not the end of the world. If everything else went okay, I still had plenty of time to heed my friend's warning.

But everything else did not go okay. While the flight south was smooth enough, thunderheads were waiting for us in the distance. Skirting the Big Island's windward side, we dropped down through dense cloud and landed in blinding rain, the kind of downpour Hilo is famous for. My rental car was ready. The roads

27

were not. You couldn't see five metres in front of you. I'd never known that kind of rain. I should have pulled over and waited a while. I kept thinking it would let up. How could there be enough water in the heavens to sustain this kind of deluge for more than ten minutes? What's more, I thought I knew where I was going, having flown into Hilo once before, years earlier, on a day when the skies were clear.

I must have been half an hour from the airport when I realised I'd taken a wrong turn, maybe two wrong turns. I was lost again, disoriented this time, and running out of patience with myself. As the rains at last began to subside, a parting in the clouds sent down a dome of muted light that fell upon a cluster of shops at the end of a low-slung town. All but one of the shops looked closed, perhaps abandoned. At a corner of the parking lot stood a phone booth. I pulled in close and jumped out, taking a moment to study the sky. In the tropics, night comes early, and in this kind of weather, things could shut down fast. But I can't be that far away, I told myself. I still had time.

I dialled his number and heard ten rings before I hung up. After missing the first flight, I'd called from Honolulu. Depending on the weather, he'd said, he might try to meet me 'up above', meaning where the asphalt ended. By this time that's probably where he was, waiting up above, a mile from his house.

So now what? Don't panic. That store looks open. Just walk over there and ask for directions. Yes, that's easy enough. But first you'd better lock the car.

I shoved a hand into my trousers pocket, only to discover an emptiness where the keys should have been. I checked inside the booth – on the floor, on the shelf below the phone. I tried the driver's door which, incredibly, was already locked. How could I have locked the door? At a glance I could see that all the doors were locked, all the windows were up, and there were the keys, one in the ignition switch, the other dangling like a tiny silver charm inside the claw machine at the county fair, the prize you'll never reach.

How could this happen? Was there some button I had pushed, or failed to push? It had been ten years since I'd locked myself out of a car, and here I was – no tools, miles from the rental office, at the arse-end of some Big Island road, with the sun going down and more rain on its way. As the long day of mishaps caught up with me, I was suddenly exhausted, overwhelmed. I would have to do something – smash in a window or call the agency and wait two hours for a tow truck – but I needed a moment of calm, to restore my will. I leaned and placed my forehead against the car's roof – the cool and glossy curve – trying not to be defeated by a pattern of oversights and costly lapses I could now trace back to junior high. As I stood there contemplating the folly of my entire life, a voice from somewhere behind me spoke one word.

'Eh.'

I turned and saw a huge Polynesian fellow, Hawaiian or perhaps, from the size of him, Samoan. His dark features were etched and fierce. Black hair was drawn back into a stubby knot. His mouth arced in what seemed a permanent scowl, as he regarded me in the twilight of this otherwise empty parking lot.

I was thinking, Oh shit! This was exactly what you heard about. A rental car. An island visitor. Alone. At night. Somewhere in the back country. On the wrong road or the wrong beach. While seductive ads called Hawaii 'The Paradise of the Pacific', many locals had come to see escalating tourism as a threat and a scourge. Just the previous week, according to the Honolulu paper, a young French couple had been robbed at a remote camping site and beaten senseless with baseball bats. Was this to be my penance?

I glanced past him, wondering if there were others, though he didn't need any others. His brown arms, purpled with tattoos, were the size of my legs. His thighs were as thick as nail kegs. He outweighed me by fifty kilos, and it wasn't fat. If he came at me, I was finished. All his life he had hated white guys, and now he had one at his mercy. I could try to outrun him, but where would I run to? Given my luck on this particular day, I'd probably run right into the jaws of something worse.

I had already surrendered, reaching for my wallet to offer what I had, when his warrior face opened in a large smile, amused and incongruously youthful.

'Eh, you need one coat hangah?'

'Coat hanger?' I said weakly, as if he'd asked me to approve his weapon of choice.

'For stick inside da window.'

'Oh right. Good.' Relief poured through me like rainwater. 'A coat hanger. Yes, that is just what I need.'

'Maybe I got one. Lemme go check 'em out.'

He wore *zori* slippers, baggy shorts and a vast blue-and-white aloha shirt, and moved like a sumo wrestler, arms pushed away from his body by slabs of muscle and flesh.

In my haste I hadn't noticed his car, parked in shadows near a leafy and neglected hedge – a long-hooded Ford Fairlane once painted green, so riddled with rust holes large and small you might think someone had used it for target practice.

Opening the trunk he rummaged through a clutter of automotive debris and emerged with a wire coat hanger. As he lumbered toward me his thick hands straightened it.

'Found 'em,' he said.

'You're saving my life.'

'No big thing.'

After shaping a tiny hook at one end, he selected a window that was not shut tight and forced the wire over the top edge. Once it was inside he wriggled it back and forth, fashioning curves and angles as it descended, until he had the hook around the little tube that clicks up and down to lock and unlock the door. He moved with such speed and dexterity it was clear he had wide experience in the techniques of liberating vehicles. I gave a prayer of thanks that he hadn't come upon my car parked somewhere out by itself and unattended. I watched his nimble fingers tug and lift until the latch clicked.

With an ironic grin he handed me the wire. 'You wanna keep this? Just in case?'

'Maybe I should hang onto it. I still don't know how this happened.'

'Where you going anyhow?'

I told him the name of the road I'd been searching for.

'Right on my way,' he said. 'You like follow me?'

Under darkening skies his heavy features, for an instant, seemed menacing again. Anxiety came rising up, a lingering flicker of paranoia, as it occurred to me that this might not be a rescue after all, but some ploy to lure me out of the parking lot and farther down a road of no return.

I almost said no, I could find it on my own. But that boyish smile lit up his face – a welcoming smile is what it was, a forgiving smile – and then I wanted to hug him. Maybe I should have. I thanked him again, told him I'd buy him a beer.

Nodding in a way that did not mean yes and did not mean no, he said, 'Hey, one time maybe I get stuck, you come by, do da same. Everything come round, you know.'

He bunched his thick brow with a glance into the dusk, and spoke as if prompted by something unseen, over there at the edge of darkness.

'Dey call it da Big Island. But it's not that big. Everything come round and round and round.'

Easing into the Fairlane, he had to sit down sideways, then turn and squeeze his immense frame behind the steering wheel. The engine roared to life and I followed him out of the parking lot, into the wild and sultry night.

One Night in the Sahara

AMANDA JONES

Amanda Jones is a freelance travel writer and photographer from New Zealand who now lives in the
San Francisco Bay Area. Her work appears in *Travel
& Leisure*, the *Los Angeles Times*, the *London
Sunday Times*, *Vogue* and *Condé Nast Traveller*,
among other publications. Between trips she jug-
gles the mother-worker paradigm and dreams of
the Sahara.

I REMEMBER ONE NIGHT in particular when a man with whom I could not speak saved me.

I was in the Sahara Desert, travelling with a group of people I neither knew nor liked especially well. We were en route to a Tuareg wedding, moving via jeep during the day and sleeping under the stars at night. It was arduous travel. The daytime heat was stupefying and the drives were long, with nothing to do but stare morosely at the passing desert.

I would wait for the nights with their cooling air, the gloom relieving the sun, the moon hovering huge and the Milky Way luminous. And each evening, after my companions ate dinner and retired to their mattresses, I would leave on a walk.

That night I left camp at about nine, foolishly dressed only in a thin cotton shirt and light trousers. The sky was inky and the moon had arced high, casting a meek metallic light on the ground. But the desert seemed radiant and beckoning, and I was overjoyed to be alone and moving.

After an hour of euphoric ambling, I finally turned back towards camp. It was not until that moment that I realised how far I had come and that I had no idea where I was. I looked for footprints, but beneath my feet was hard-baked earth – flat and stony. With horror I realised there were no landmarks and I had left no trail.

Resisting panic, I looked to the sky as I imagined one is supposed to do in such situations – and found I was, of course, utterly clueless about celestial navigation. As I stumbled onward I was reminded of a game I had once played with a Tuareg guide in the Western Sahara. He had delighted in taking off one of his many scarves, wrapping it around my eyes, leading me in a straight line, then telling me to find my way back, blindfolded, to the starting place. It seemed easy enough, child's play, but I was hopeless, repeatedly veering off course. The more certain I was of my direction, the more wrong I was, as if the desert itself was conspiring against me. My stately, indigo-shrouded guide had laughed at me, then had me spin him in circles before performing the task himself. On every occasion he strode back to the starting spot without faltering. When

I asked how he had learned this trick, he replied, 'It is no trick. It is the most important rule of the desert. You must learn to watch, to be sure and always remember where you have come from.'

And so I had broken the cardinal rule of the desert. The flamboyance of my stupidity dawned on me. I was a city girl who fancied herself an adventurer and now I was lost with no water, no food and no warmth. It was almost comical in its cliché.

The cold had descended and I shook, Sahara nights being as brutally frigid as the days are blisteringly hot. As I lurched over the featureless land, I knew my fellow travellers would be sleeping and there would be no light coming from our encampment. I could stumble within ten metres of them without knowing it.

I'd been searching for a good hour when I turned and saw a smudge of fire glowing in the distance. After an initial rush of relief, I froze, realising my predicament. Here I was, a youngish blond woman alone at night, lost and desperate. Tuareg rebels ranged throughout the area and they were armed, angry and not known for their tenderness towards women.

However, having little choice, I walked towards the glow with as much assurance as I could muster. As I came closer I recognised the figure of a Wodaabe tribesman, his lean body draped in white robes, face encircled by a turban, aquiline features etched by the penumbral firelight.

The Wodaabe are nomads of the Sahel, the rocky scrublands that signal the beginning of the Sahara. I had spent time with the Wodaabe in the past and I knew they were magnificently gracious people, beautiful to regard, proud of their heritage and impeccably hospitable. They do, however, have quite liberal sexual practices and an unsettling tendency to request sex of a woman by scratching her inner palm. The woman is expected to follow the scratcher then and there behind a bush – although, thankfully, the Wodaabe have great respect for women and typically accept rejection with a shrug.

As I approached, the man looked up in surprise. I must have made a shocking vision: a lone woman staggering from the darkness wearing safari pants and hiking boots. Previously, when I had camped with a Wodaabe tribe, the women had not hesitated to tell me how peculiar and unappealing it was that I wore men's clothing. With unabashed candour they had also informed me that although my long, straight hair and high cheekbones were somewhat attractive, and that my height and long limbs were good, the blondness of my hair, the paleness of my green eyes and the whiteness of my skin rendered me substantially less than desirable. Being considered ugly, I factored, could now only work to my advantage.

I extended my hand to the man mumbling '*Foma, foma, foma*', the Wodaabe Fulfulde greeting which means 'Hello, how are you, your family, your goats, your camels, your donkeys?' That, sadly, was the extent of my Fulfulde. I spoke again in hesitant French, knowing that many Wodaabe spoke the colonial language of West Africa. He shook his head, indicating he didn't understand, but took my hand and led me to the fire, gesturing for me to sit on the ground. He had a fresh pot of the sweet tea that the Wodaabe have adopted from North Africa. He poured me a glass, speaking soothingly in Fulfulde. It was my turn to shake my head.

Nearby, a bellicose gargle issued from the dark. I looked over and made out the figure of a recumbent camel beneath an acacia tree. The man rose and went to the camel, returning with a cotton cloth which he placed around my shoulders.

Wodaabe are officially Muslims, although they, like the Tuaregs, have their own interpretation of Islam. They wear the voluminous robes of desert dwellers – designed to capture and swirl air around the skin – but it is the men who cover their heads, not the women. Good looks are highly esteemed, and they are in fact a striking people – tall, thin, mocha-skinned and fine-featured.

My rescuer looked to be in his thirties. His eyes were widely spaced, almond shaped and molten brown. I gazed at him, knowing that it mattered how sure of myself I was. If I seemed fearful, he might consider taking advantage of the situation. I spoke to him in English and French, aware it was useless, but gesturing blindly into the darkness to indicate I was lost and needed to find my camp. He stared at me sagely, although I had no idea what, if anything, he understood. He made no movement other than squatting on his haunches and pouring tea from high above the glass, returning the first serving back to the pot, as is tradition, then pouring again until the amber liquid frothed.

I stopped speaking entirely and felt the immensity of the desert. I looked about me and understood that this would be a memory that would exist in me forever. I saw myself, finally warm beside this fire, drinking tea with a stranger with whom I shared no more than two common words. My life was as odd to him as his was to me. In all likelihood he had never ridden in a car, had never seen a city, knew nothing of computers or telephones. Yet it was his knowledge I now needed, my own more modern skills having proved useless. And what I needed most was for him to be kind to me.

After some time of drinking tea in silence, my host rose, checked the tether on his camel and beckoned to me. I folded the borrowed cloth and followed the softly billowing whiteness of his robes into the night. We walked in quiet, although at times I would burst into speech, feeling awkward with such great silence in the presence of another. He would turn and smile but say nothing, continuing to move effortlessly over the stony earth.

Several times he stopped and took my hand. When he first did this I tensed, anticipating the scratch of the palm. But it never came. We just walked like that, hand in hand, and quickly the oddity faded. Wodaabe and Tuareg men hold hands quite comfortably, and I knew it did not have the same romantic implications as in our culture.

Within thirty minutes a cluster of mosquito nets loomed not three metres in front, and then the humped shapes of the sleeping bodies beneath them. His finding this small encampment in the dark seemed to me utterly miraculous.

I turned to him, put my hand over my heart and said the only other word I knew in Fulfulde: '*Abarkidi*'. Thank you. He laughed, his perfect teeth gleaming, then covered his heart and backed away, raising both hands upward in farewell. I stood still and watched until the desert night reclaimed him.

Tea and Cheese in Turkey

ALICE WATERS

Alice Waters is the owner of Chez Panisse restaurant in Berkeley, California. Over the last three decades, Chez Panisse has cultivated a network of local farmers who share the restaurant's commitment to sustainable agriculture. In 2001, Chez Panisse was named best restaurant in the United States by *Gourmet* magazine. Alice Waters initiated the edible schoolyard project in 1995; this program incorporates her ideas about food and culture into the public school curriculum. She is the author of eight books, the most recent of which is *Chez Panisse Fruit*.

I HAVE TOLD THIS STORY many, many times. It's the story I always tell. The trouble is, I'm not a very good storyteller, and I don't remember background details very well. And for me to get the point of this story across you really have to be right in front of me so I can give you something to eat. But I'll try.

This was in my early twenties, after I graduated from college in Berkeley. It was the summer after I completed Montessori training in London and I had decided I was going to be a teacher. I was driving across Turkey with my friend Judy Johnson in a tiny beat-up Morris Minor. A couple of friendly young Frenchmen were covering the same route, shadowing us in another car. They were both named Jean-something, I think. None of us spoke Turkish. Actually, none of us knew much about Turks or Turkish history. We were just curious and tried to be polite.

God knows they were polite to us! Much more than polite, in fact. The Turks were hospitable in a way that made the mythical come alive. It was as though we were living that beautiful story of Baucis and Philemon who took in Zeus and Hermes when they were visiting earth disguised as travellers. They gave us the very best of everything they had. Once, I'll never forget, when we were camping out in the countryside near some goatherds, we woke up in the morning to find that a bowl of fresh goat's milk had been slipped under the door-flap of our little tent while we slept. This is how we were treated everywhere. In one village we were conscripted into a wedding celebration, and Judy and I helped adorn the bride while the Frenchmen drank with the men. We all feasted and danced for three days.

From Turkey we went on to Corfu, where we lived for a while on practically nothing, watching the sun and the moon rising and setting over the Aegean. We ate fish fresh out of the sunstruck sea and picked fruit ripening under the brilliant sky. For the first time in my life, I was unmistakably part of the natural rhythm of a place, and life itself seemed entirely worth living.

But the story I started out to tell happened on the way to

Cappadocia, in Central Anatolia. This was over thirty years ago, but there were driveable roads all the way. It was not a particularly adventurous or out-of-the-way destination, but even so, this was long before *Star Wars* was filmed there and before innkeepers in the conical cave-dwellings of Göreme had Internet access. The road was long, hot, dusty, little-trafficked and very sparsely populated.

And then we ran out of petrol. Or at any rate, the tank was so low that we could not safely go any farther, so we pulled up at the only petrol station for miles and miles. There was a petrol pump, and a little building and an oil company sign. The Frenchmen pulled in behind us after a few minutes and their tank was low too. A shy, big-eyed boy appeared, nine or ten years old and wearing an embroidered cap, and he mimed that there was no petrol to pump. And we counter-mimed that we supposed we would have to wait. Would that be all right? There was petrol on the way, wasn't there? Then, fingers pointing to mouth, where could we get something to eat?

This is the part of my story I have to act out to make you understand. Solemnly the boy leads us indoors and into the back room where there are benches against the wall covered with beautiful old rugs, a brazier in the corner made out of an old petrol can, birdcages hanging from the low ceiling, and a baby brother. Clearly the parents are away and the big brother has been left behind to baby-sit and turn away customers, and to offer us the imperative hospitality of rural Turkey.

The boy builds a fire out of pine cones, puts on a kettle and makes us tea. Then he produces a small piece of cheese and painstakingly cuts it into even smaller pieces, which he offers us gravely. We drink the tea and eat the tiny pieces of dry cheese.

And that's all that happens in this story.

Crassly, we asked if there was anything else to eat, and there wasn't, and we waited for hours and hours, wondering if the parents would ever come back. I remember sleeping on the carpeted bench. We eventually flagged down a passing trucker and persuaded him to let us siphon some of his petrol so we could drive on.

But in the important part of the story, all that happens is the birdcages hang from the ceiling and the boy makes us tea and intently shares his meagre lunch. We realise he has given us everything he has, and he has done this with absolutely no expectation of anything in return. That's all. A small miracle of trust and a lesson in hospitality that changed my life forever.

In the myth, Zeus and Hermes are so touched by the generosity of Philemon and Baucis that the poor old couple is granted their wish to die together, their humble cottage is transformed into a temple, and they are turned into an oak tree and a linden tree. But all who offer sacred hospitality are rewarded in the very same way: our dwellings become as temples and our branches intertwine.

A Bowl of Soup, in a Basket

BETH KEPHART

Beth Kephart is the award-winning author of three memoirs: *A Slant of Sun*, *Into the Tangle of Friendship* and *Still Love in Strange Places*.' Frequently anthologised, her essays, profiles and reviews have appeared in the *New York Times*, the *Washington Post*, the *Chicago Tribune*, *Real Simple*, *Parenting*, Salon.com and elsewhere. Her new book of nonfiction will be published in 2004.

I NEVER PHOTOGRAPHED LUIS; I have no record of his face. I didn't memorise his room beyond the shadow colour of its walls and the cage of parakeets that hung from a hook near his bed. One of the birds was yellow and one of the birds was green, and the cage itself was polished or perhaps limned by the few available threads of sun that slipped in through his courtyard window.

Was it like this? Were Luis's eyes grey and his body impoverished by time, and did we once find him asleep on his narrow cot when we arrived with a bag of tomatoes? Luis was old and he wasn't well. He divided the hours of his day into sleeping and cooking, then promising his birds the whistle of a song.

Luis wasn't related to me by blood; in fact, I hardly knew him. But he was like a grandfather to my brother-in-law, who lived one floor above him in a building in Seville, off the Plaza de Santa Isabel, where the nuns floated on a sea of black habits, and the ornamental orange trees displayed their bitter fruits, and the double amputee sat on the throne of his wheelchair, strumming his guitar. The building was ancient, not fashionably so, but it offered a view from the upper-floor balconies and a hearty rendering of the hour from the bell tower next door. In my brother-in-law's apartment there was a mousetrap by the kitchen sink and a live mouse in the bathtub. The shower water was a laconic brown trickle and the tile floor was busted to pieces. But in addition to the balcony that faced out towards the plaza there was the kitchen window that faced in, towards the courtyard. It was through this window that my brother-in-law, Rodi, would call to his almost-grandfather, Luis, and through which Luis would call back up to him: suggestions for a recipe; a comment on a bullfight; something about the birds. Or so it seemed.

During my first trip to Seville, in September of 1993, I was assaulted by bouts of claustrophobia. Rodi's apartment, for one thing, was hardly large enough to accommodate my husband, myself and our four-year-old son, not to mention Rodi himself. Still, there we were – the three of us assigned to Rodi's one bed and Rodi assigned to the apartment's single couch, a dilapidated, melodramatic creature that was swathed in several layers of Gypsy fabric. For meals we sat around a table designed for two, and when it was time to take our showers we struggled to win the favour of that trickle.

Seville itself seemed like a city of divergences – the main roads slivered like alleys, and the alleys were nothing but halved pavements, and the pavements themselves were so infinitesimal that stray cats could be seen slipping off the curbs. You had to strain your neck to find the sky, and you could easily get lost, as I did on the second morning of our first visit, when I left the apartment in search of air as the others tossed with sleep.

I don't know where I thought I was headed or why I assumed that I'd find my way back. I passed bakeries, selling flat sticks of bread; vendors; the smell of marmalade. I walked by houses, all in a row, connected. I took refuge in doorways when scooters fumed by; passed women nursing children, girls playing with dolls, thin men reading newspapers, swollen old maids tipping watering cans into the plants that grew out of the huge ceramic pots that decorated the courtyards I could just barely glimpse beyond the gates. One street led to another, until I lost all sense of where I was and didn't know north from south, east from west, this reflective church steeple from the other. Where was the river? Where was the train station or the Plaza de Santa Isabel? Where was the man with the magazines?

There's no real option when you're lost and can't speak the language but to keep walking and to pray for the familiar. So I kept walking through Seville that morning, until I found myself in a neighbourhood unlike the others, where the women were just home from their night at work and stood in clusters smoking cigarettes, bored, it seemed to me, with one another.

It was here, in this neighbourhood that I have never found again, that I saw what I have never since forgotten. Looking through a set of gates into a cloistered courtyard I saw a group of young boys playing what looked to be a game, until I was close enough to stare. There were six boys in all, and each looked much like the other, with black hair cut straight across the brow and copper flecks in the brown of the eyes. Five of them ran in a circle around the sitting sixth, the youngest. 'Duck, duck, goose,' I thought I heard them sing, but what a stupid supposition, for as I stood there watching on the street side of the gate, four of the running boys pitched a scream then threw themselves upon the youngest. Each took a separate limb of him and flipped him from his haunches to his stomach, pinning him to the ground and spreading him apart, as if he were a matted butterfly. When the victim was arranged to the tallest one's approval, he – the tallest one – snatched something pale and plastic from his sleeve. He pointed it up into the air like a dagger, then jammed it down to the seam of the youngest's pants, over and again. The screaming stays with me. The screaming and how I, standing on the opposite side of that gate, did nothing at all to intervene.

A city can give you a fever. Disgust has the biology of a virus. I can't remember how I found my way back to Plaza de Santa Isabel – what alley I followed, which ribbon of sky – but I know I said nothing of what I had seen, just kept it seething inside me, contained. Nor do I know how long it took before I got sick in a tangible, external way, but within a few days I could not leave that apartment. My husband and his brother would go out at night, and my son and I would stay counting the bell chimes. Or listening to the guitarist as he strummed his songs, or to the feet of the nuns inside their habits. Seville, a city I would someday fall so deeply in love with that I would try to make it real inside a novel, had not yet invited me in. I hadn't yet seen the lizards on the walls at night. I hadn't yet sat outside at midnight, with wine and tapas. I hadn't yet lost myself to the sound of flamenco, or put out my hand for the tossed candy of Christmas, or photographed children dancing on an adjacent rooftop, or shopped for a fresh chicken in the market, or walked across the bridge to Triana. I hadn't found Seville, not yet, and I was far from home.

But downstairs Luis was home, and somehow he had learned about my troubles – a conversation between windowsills, no doubt. And one afternoon – when I was shivering, listless and lonesome – I learned that Luis had sent a bowl of soup my way. He had, in other words, called for the rope and the basket that Rodi had rigged between their windows, saying 'Send the basket down, kid,' or something like that. He had ladled his broth into a bowl, nested the bowl inside the basket and hollered for Rodi to start pulling. The basket with the bowl of soup went from one window to another, and then it came to me.

What we don't know about kindness is where to look for it, how to hope for it, in a city full of strangers. We don't know how the man downstairs who doesn't speak our language divines just what we need or even, perhaps, what we've seen. 'Many thanks,' I hope I called down to Luis, or, at least, I hope Rodi called for me. 'Many thanks, the soup is good.'

What do you trade for a bowl of soup? Perhaps a bag of tomatoes, if you're lucky.

What I tried to do, but I never did it well, was make Luis the hero of a novel. I tried to give him an adolescence during the Spanish Civil War and a half-brother he loved named Miguel. I tried to make the flamenco stomp through him and to give him a woman to remember. I tried to let him die in the company of a cook I named Stella, on a *cortijo* where the olives rained from trees.

But the truth is, real men are better than their fictions. The truth is, you cannot return a bowl of soup to a man who has passed on. For Luis, when I met him, was dying; leukaemia would win its battle soon. Luis was dying when he made me a bowl of soup. He wasn't well enough to leave his darkened room, but he had time to nest a cure inside a basket.

We go far away and we try to bring home the things we believe we must remember. From Seville, during that trip, I brought home tapestry and porcelain, miniature bullfighters and a Spanish barrette for my hair. I brought postcards and books and photographs, but I have no record of Luis's face. All I have now is the colour of his room and the fidelity of the birds inside their cage. All I have is how I imagined him afterwards, and the startling honest truth about a bowl of soup.

Highland Remedy

FRAN PALUMBO

Born on Columbus Day, Fran Palumbo has jour-
neyed around the world indulging in a lifelong
compulsion to explore. Recently unshackled
from her day job, she aspires to visit the places in
the world she has not yet been and to pursue a
career in freelance writing. This is her first published work.

THE SCENERY MIRRORS my own interior landscape: grey, drizzly, melancholy. Even though it's rained every day since I arrived a week ago, I find it difficult to dislike this place. Light mist coats the austere, rolling terrain, giving it the soft, delicate appearance of a giant pastel. Throughout the day the sun pokes through occasionally and an ivory northern light illuminates a distant hill or a crumbling stone wall as if the entrance to Camelot lies ahead. Zooming northeast on Route A9 from Inverness to Wick, I shift the gears of the red subcompact rental car, left-handed, as if I've been driving on the other side of the road my entire bloody life. What better place to hide away from the world than the Scottish Highlands?

Following three turbulent months in India, I decided to make an impromptu detour to Scotland on the way back to San Francisco. My mind was still whirling from the too recent past of sweltering heat, despicable filth, abject poverty, utter chaos and claustrophobic hordes of people. My stomach was still churning from the parasite that had maliciously hitched a ride in my bowels. A perhaps irreconcilable rift with my best friend, who accused me of not being grateful enough for her hospitality in India, had rendered me bereft. Plus, I was still suffering from a painful failed romance that ended badly prior to my departure for Asia. It seemed as though everybody within the small solar system of my life wanted something from me. I had exceeded my tolerance level for fellow human beings. My entire body and soul reverberated with a Garboesque 'I vont to be alone!'

Now, cruising through the coastal towns of Dornoch, Brora and Dunbeath, I stop methodically to quickly snap photos or visit castle ruins noted by a miniature red star on my map. There are dozens of these freckly red stars and I am determined to see the site representing each one. This preoccupies me and helps to quiet the demon voices chattering in my head. The voices in my abdomen, however, are not so easily subdued. They let out a grotesque whine. I need to eat.

It's been a long day of driving and I plan on stopping in Wick, a town that looks like the largest one around judging from the bold typeface on the map. Upon arriving, though, I find it a dreary place except for a few historic stone buildings and a couple of geriatric-looking three-star hotels. I motor straight through, even though it's early evening and I just want to settle down with a hearty meal and comfy room.

Continuing north, the route becomes less travelled and eventually ends at Duncansby Head, the northeasternmost corner of the Scottish mainland where the harbour village of John o'Groats squats humbly in its midst. This windswept piece of Scotland is empty and flat, nothing but land, sky and water punctuated by a stiff seaborne breeze. From here you can catch a ferry in the summer to the Orkney Islands, but other than that, it barely deserves a dot on the map. There's no homey brick B & Bs, no discernable centre of town. Across the road from each other are two rectangular fifties-style motels, about half a kilometre from the water where only a few boats are docked. A caravan park sits oddly off to the right with several large vehicles parked randomly like perverse modern-day monoliths. Worse yet, there isn't a restaurant in sight. This feels like the loneliest place on earth.

I look at the map, and the next town appears to be far away. The type is too small. It might not even have a place to stay. I reluctantly check into the Seaview Motel and drop my suitcase in the room. One tiny window looks out onto the deserted road, and a lumpy double bed covered by a chenille bedspread patterned in pink, green and white sits against the wall in the middle of the room. Hanging over the bed there's a tacky, faded print of a cherub holding a fishing pole. John o'Groats is not the charming place I'd hoped to hunker down in for a good dinner and a night's rest.

Directed by the motel desk clerk to a place a kilometre back that might still be serving dinner, I wearily head off in the car again. At least it hasn't rained in a few hours. Peeking through dark, pregnant clouds the summer sun glows stubbornly, descending toward the ground in a slow, languid motion. I am so far north it won't get dark until around 11 p.m.

Arriving at a modest building that looks like it might have been a small church in a previous incarnation, I walk in and head to the counter to order some food. In thick chalk letters, a blackboard menu overhead offers burgers, sandwiches and soup. The room is spartan and honest like a Quaker meeting room; the odour and hiss of fried food from the kitchen hangs in the air. I order the fish and chips, make a mental note to eat healthy tomorrow, and take a seat where the cheerful husband and wife owners direct me among the few tables scattered on the hardwood floor. The only other customer – an elfish, white-haired man in dark, baggy trousers and a windbreaker, who looks to be in his seventies – smiles shyly at me from the next table.

'Aye.' He nods in my direction. I nod back.

'You're not from around here, are ye?'

'No,' I confess. 'From California. Just here travelling.' Damn. I was hoping to blend in with the locals so no one would bother me. But at least I can understand him. Most of the Scots I've talked to, although only briefly, sound as if their tongues are always getting in the way of what they're trying to say.

'So, are ye plannin' to take the ferry to the Orkneys?'

'Well, no, I hadn't really thought about it. I'm just driving. Didn't think there was much to see there.'

'Well, y'ought to consider it. Last year I was here and took the ferry on o'r and spent the day. It was lovely.'

He launches into a guidebook-like monologue about the birdwatching and ancient sites – something called the Ring of Brodgar. I am given directions and details on the ferry schedule and how to get to the attractions. Even though I know I won't go, I feign interest and make conversation as though I really want all this information. In fact, I don't even want to talk to him. I want to eat in silence, want to listen to all the activity going on in my head. This friendly chitchat is wearing me out, but he's such a nice, pleasant man that I talk to him anyway. He's alone. He's probably lonely.

A huge platter of fish and chips is placed in front of me and I can't shove the crispy brown chunks into my mouth fast enough.

After a few minutes, as if not wanting to interrupt my eating, the old man rises from his table and, with a slight bow and twinkle in his eye, shakes my hand and tells me he enjoyed talking with me.

It's getting late and I want to get back to the motel, take a walk down to the water and catch the sunset, so I devour the rest of the meal and head up to the counter to pay. The owner waves away the bills I hold out.

'It's paid for,' he tells me. I am confused.

'The ol' man paid for you when he left.'

Amazed that a stranger would pay for my dinner then leave without any acknowledgement of his kindness, I smile and think, 'How sweet.' No one has ever done this before in any of my travels, and I am incredibly touched. All of these months, after feeling as though every single person I encountered was a living, breathing 'give-me' machine, I meet one person in a remote corner of the world who gives just for the sake of giving, wanting nothing in return, not even a 'thank you'. This small gesture is, ironically, larger than he will ever know. I have an inexplicable urge to find the old man, a desperate need to thank him. I don't even know his name.

Sure enough, way up ahead on the side of the road, I spot his dark silhouette shuffling along, hands in his pockets. 'Would you like a ride?' I ask, pulling up beside him. His face lights up in a broad smile and he eagerly accepts the offer. He is short and agile and has a perky, turned-up nose. For a moment I think that maybe I've encountered a leprechaun, but then realise I'm in the wrong country for such occurrences, even if they were possible. I drive back to my motel, park the car and we stroll side by side toward the water, to the coastline of Pentland Firth, which separates the mainland from the Orkneys.

His name is Walter. He's from Newcastle, a city just below the Scottish border, and is staying at the caravan park. As if reading my mind, he comments matter-of-factly, 'My wife, she died a few years back,' and his face becomes as wistful and lonely as the Highland landscape itself. For a moment, I have another silly thought: I wish

I was seventy so that Walter and I could tour around Scotland in his mobile home for the rest of our lives. He touches my arm and points to something a few hundred metres away.

An old Victorian hotel I hadn't noticed before sits way off in the shadows looking haunted near the shoreline. 'It's been closed for many years,' Walter tells me. He travels often to John o'Groats, and as I look around I begin to understand why. The sun dangles low in the sky as if trying to prolong its inevitable kiss with the horizon. Wide, dramatic stalks of light radiate through billowy clouds, providing an ethereal backdrop for a distant house sitting squarely on a desolate plain. The house looks how I feel: forlorn and alone, but illuminated. Standing there together we are an unlikely pair, yet are kindred spirits, drawn to the healing power that blows in from the frigid, ancient waters.

Mesmerised, we watch the sun as it gradually extinguishes itself into the edge of the world. Sometimes the best conversations occur with strangers, without words. Here, with Walter, my faith in humanity might just be restored.

Looking for Abdelati

TANYA SHAFFER

Tanya Shaffer is the author of *Somebody's Heart is Burning: A Woman Wanderer in Africa*. Her stories have appeared on Salon.com, in *Speakeasy* magazine and in numerous anthologies. An actor as well as a writer, she has toured nationally and internationally with her solo shows *Let My Enemy Live Long!* and *Miss America's Daughters* and her original play *Brigadista*. Visit her online at www.tanyashaffer.com.

HERE'S WHAT I LOVE about travel: strangers get a chance to amaze you. Sometimes a single day can bring a blooming surprise, a simple kindness that opens a chink in the brittle shell of your heart and makes you a different person when you go to sleep – more tender, less jaded – than the one you were when you woke up.

This particular day began when Miguel and I descended from a cramped, cold bus at 7 a.m. and walked the stinking grey streets of Casablanca with our backpacks, looking for food. Six days earlier I had finished a stint on a volunteer project, creating a public park in Kenitra, an ugly industrial city on the Moroccan coast. This was my final day of travel before hopping a plane to sub-Saharan Africa and more volunteer work.

Miguel was one of five non-Moroccans on the work project, a 21-year-old vision of flowing brown curls and buffed golden physique. Although having him as a travelling companion took care of any problems I might have encountered with Moroccan men, he was inordinately devoted to his girlfriend, Eva, a wonderfully brassy, wiry, chain-smoking Older Woman of twenty-five with a husky Scotch-drinker's voice, whom he couldn't go more than half an hour without mentioning. Unfortunately, Eva had had to head back to Barcelona immediately after the three-week work camp ended, and Miguel wanted to explore Morocco. Since I was the only other person on the project who spoke Spanish, and he spoke no French or Arabic, his tight orbit shifted onto me, and we became travelling companions. This involved posing as a married couple at hotels, which made Miguel so uncomfortable that the frequency of his references to Eva went from half-hour to fifteen-minute intervals, and then five as we got closer to bedtime. Finally one night, as we set up in our room in Fès, I took him by the shoulders and said, 'Miguel, it's okay. You're a handsome man, but I'm over twenty-one. I can handle myself, I swear.'

This morning we were going to visit Abdelati, a sweet, gentle young man we'd worked with on the project in Kenitra. He'd been expecting us to arrive in Casablanca for a few days, and since he had no telephone, he'd written down his address and told us to just show up – his mother and sisters were always at home. Since my plane was leaving from Casablanca the following morning, we wanted to get an early start so we could spend the whole day with him.

Unlike the romantic image its name conjured, Casablanca was a thoroughly modern city, with rectangular high-rises sprouting everywhere and wide boulevards already jammed with cars. Horns blared, and the air was thick with heat and exhaust. My T-shirt, pinned to my skin by my backpack, was soaked with sweat. Eventually we scored some croissants and overly sugared *panaches* (a mix of banana, apple and orange juice) at a roadside café, where the friendly proprietor advised us to take a taxi rather than a bus out to Abdelati's neighbourhood. He said the taxi should cost about twenty dirham – under three dollars – and the buses would take all day.

It took us an hour to find a cab. When we did, the poker-faced driver informed us that the address which Abdelati had written down for us was somehow suspect. When we got to the neighbourhood, he told us, we would have to ask directions.

'Here we go,' Miguel whispered, rolling his eyes. 'Eva would hate this.'

First the driver asked a cop, who scratched his head and asked our nationalities, looking at our grimy faces and scraggly attire with bemused tolerance. After more small talk, he pointed vaguely to a park a few blocks away. There a group of barefoot seven- or eight-year-old boys were kicking a soccer ball. Our driver asked where Abdelati's house was and one of the boys said Abdelati had moved, but he could take us to the new house.

This seemed a bit odd to me, since Abdelati had just given me the address a week ago, but since a similar thing had happened in Fès, I chalked it up as another Moroccan mystery and didn't worry about it too much.

The little boy came with us in the cab, full of his own importance, squirming and twisting to wave at other children as we inched down the narrow, winding roads. Finally the little boy pointed to a house, and our driver went to the door and inquired. He came back to the cab saying Abdelati's sister was in this house visiting friends and would come along to show us where they lived.

Soon a lovely, delicate-featured girl of about sixteen emerged from the house. She was dressed in a Western skirt and blouse, which surprised me since Abdelati's strong religious beliefs and upright demeanour had made me think he came from a more traditional family. Another thing that surprised me was her skin colour. Whereas Abdelati looked very African, this young woman was an olive-skinned Arab. Still, I'd seen other unusual familial combinations in Morocco's complex racial mosaic, so I didn't give it too much thought.

We soon arrived at another house where Abdelati's sister directed our taxi driver to stop. We waited in the front yard while the sister went in and returned accompanied by her mother, sisters and brother-in-law, all of whom greeted us with cautious warmth. Unlike the younger girl, the older sisters wore traditional robes, though their faces were not veiled. You see a range of orthodoxy in Moroccan cities, caught as they are between Europe and the Arab world. From the younger sister's skirt and blouse to the completely veiled women gliding through the streets with only their eyes in view, the women's outfits embody the entire spectrum.

We paid our taxi driver, and I tipped and thanked him profusely, until he grew embarrassed and drove away.

We were ushered into a pristine middle-class Moroccan home, with an intricately carved doorway and swirling multicoloured tiles lining the walls. The mother told us in broken French that Abdelati was out, but would be home soon. We sat on low, cushioned seats in the living room, drinking sweet, pungent mint tea poured at a suitable height from a tiny silver teapot and eating sugar cookies, while the family members took turns sitting with us and making shy, polite conversation that frequently lapsed into uncomfortable silence. Every time anything was said, Miguel would say '*Qué pasó?*' with extreme eagerness, and I would translate the mundane fragment into Spanish for him: 'Nice weather today. Tomorrow perhaps rain.' At this he'd sink back into fidgety frustration, undoubtedly wishing Eva were there.

An hour passed, and as the guard kept changing, more family members emerged from inner rooms. I was again struck by the fact that they were all light-skinned Arabs. How did Abdelati fit into this picture? Was he adopted? I was very curious to find out.

After two hours had passed with no sign of Abdelati, the family insisted on serving us a meal of couscous and fish. The food was a delectable blend of sweet and savoury, with plump raisins, cayenne pepper, slivered almonds and loads of garlic.

'Soon,' was the only response I got when I inquired as to what time he might arrive.

'You come to the *hammam*, the bath,' the younger sister said after we'd finished lunch. 'When we finish, he is back.'

'The bath?' I asked, looking around the apartment.

The sister laughed. 'The women's bath!' she said. 'Haven't you been yet?'

She pointed at Miguel. 'He can go to the men's; it's right next door.'

'*Qué pasó?*' said Miguel anxiously, sitting up.

'She wants to take us to the baths,' I said.

A look of abject horror crossed his face. 'The-the bath?' he stammered. 'You and me?'

'Yes,' I said, smiling widely. 'Is there some problem?'

'Well . . . well . . .'

I watched his agitation build for a moment, then sighed and put my hand over his. 'Separate baths, Miguel. You with the men, me with the women.'

'Oh.' He almost giggled with relief. 'Of course.'

The women's bath consisted of three large connecting rooms, each one hotter and steamier than the last, until you could barely see a metre in front of you. The floors were filled with naked women of all ages and body types, sitting directly on the slippery tiles, washing each other with mitts made of rough washcloths. Tiny girls and babies sat in plastic buckets filled with soapy water – their own pint-sized tubs. The women carried empty buckets, swinging like elephants' trunks, to and from the innermost room where they filled them at a stone basin from a spigot of boiling water, mixing in a little cold from a neighbouring spigot to temper it.

In a culture where the body is usually covered, I was surprised by the women's absolute lack of inhibition. They sat, mostly in pairs, pouring the water over their heads with small plastic pitchers, then scrubbing each other's backs – and I mean scrubbing. Over and over they attacked the same spot, as though they were trying to get out a particularly stubborn stain, leaving reddened flesh in their wake. They sprawled across each other's laps. They washed each other's fronts, backs, arms, legs. Some women washed themselves as though they were masturbating, hypnotically circling the same spot. Two tiny girls, who were about four years old, scrubbed their grandmother who lay sprawled across the floor face down. A prepubescent girl lay in her mother's lap, belly up, eyes closed, as relaxed as a cat, while her mother applied a forceful up and down stroke across the entire length of her daughter's torso. I was struck by one young woman in particular who reclined alone like a beauty queen in a tanning salon, back arched, head thrown back, right at the steamy heart of the baths, where the air was almost suffocating. She soaped her breasts in sensual circles, proudly, her stomach held in, long chestnut hair rippling down her back, a goddess in her domain.

Abdelati's sister, whose name was Samara, went at my back with her mitt, which felt like steel wool.

'Ow!' I cried out. 'Careful!'

This sent her into gales of laughter that drew the attention of the surrounding women, who saw what was happening and joined her in appreciative giggles as she continued to sandblast my skin.

'You must wash more often,' she said, pointing to the refuse of her work – little grey scrolls of dead skin that clung to my arms like lint on a sweater.

When it came time to switch roles, I tried to return the favour, but after a few moments Samara became impatient with my wimpiness and grabbed the washcloth herself, still laughing. After washing the front of her body she called over a friend to wash her back while she giggled and sang.

'What was it like in there?' asked Miguel when we met again outside. After his visit to the men's baths he looked pink and damp as a newborn, and I wondered whether his experience was anything like mine.

'I'd like to tell you all about it,' I said eagerly, 'but . . . .' I paused for emphasis, then leaned in and whispered, 'I don't think Eva would approve.'

When we got back to the house, the mother, older sister and uncle greeted us at the door.

'Please,' said the mother, 'Abdelati is here.'

'Oh, good,' I said, and for a moment, before I walked into the living room, his face danced in my mind – the warm brown eyes, the smile so shy and gentle and filled with radiant life.

We entered the lovely tiled room we'd sat in before, and a handsome young Arab man in nicely pressed Western pants and shirt came forward to shake our hands with an uncertain expression on his face.

'*Bonjour, mes amis,*' he said cautiously.

'*Bonjour,*' I smiled, slightly confused. '*Abdelati – est-ce qu'il est ici?*' Is Abdelati here?

'*Je suis Abdelati.*'

'But . . . but . . .' I looked from him to the family and then began to giggle tremulously. 'I . . . I'm sorry. I'm afraid we've made a bit of a mistake. I . . . I'm so embarrassed.'

'*Qué? Qué pasó?*' Miguel asked urgently. 'I don't understand. Where is he?'

'We got the wrong Abdelati,' I told him, then looked around at the assembled family who'd spent the better part of a day entertaining us. 'I'm afraid we don't actually know your son.'

For a split second no one said anything, and I wondered

whether I might implode right then and there and blow away like a pile of ash.

Then the uncle exclaimed heartily, '*Ce n'est pas grave!*'

'Yes,' the mother joined in. 'It doesn't matter at all. Won't you stay for dinner, please?'

I was so overwhelmed by their kindness that tears rushed to my eyes. For all they knew we were con artists, thieves, anything. Would such a thing ever happen in the US?

Still, with my plane leaving the next morning, I felt the moments I could share with the first Abdelati and his family slipping farther and farther away.

'Thank you so much,' I said fervently. 'It's been a beautiful, beautiful day, but please . . . Could you help me find this address?'

I took out the piece of paper Abdelati had given me back in Kenitra, and the new Abdelati, his uncle and his brother-in-law came forward to decipher it.

'This is Baalal Abdelati!' said the second Abdelati with surprise. 'We went to school together! He lives less than a kilometre from here. I will bring you to his house.'

And that is how it happened, that after taking photos and exchanging addresses and hugs and promises to write, Miguel and I left our new-found family and arrived at the home of our friend Abdelati as the last orange streak of sunset was fading into the indigo night. There I threw myself into the arms of that dear and lovely young man, exclaiming, 'I thought we'd never find you!'

After greetings had been offered all around, and the two Abdelatis had shared stories and laughter, we waved goodbye to our new friend Abdelati and entered a low, narrow hallway, lit by kerosene lamps.

'This is my mother,' said Abdelati.

And suddenly I found myself caught up in a crush of fabric and spice, gripped in the tight embrace of a completely veiled woman, who held me and cried over me and wouldn't let me go, just as though I were her own daughter, and not a stranger she'd never before laid eyes on in her life.

Special Delivery

LINDSY VAN GELDER

Lindsy van Gelder is chief writer at *Allure* magazine. Her work has also appeared in a schizophrenic variety of publications, including *Ms.*, *Town & Country*, *American Way*, the *Nation*, *PC*, *Real Simple*, the *New York Times*, the *New York Post*, *Rolling Stone* and *Out*. She's an unabashed Europhile who enthusiastically imbibed French wine and cheese as often as possible during the war in Iraq.

'Special Delivery' © Lindsy van Gelder 2003. First published on Salon.com and in *Salon.com's Wanderlust: Real-life Tales of Adventure and Romance*.

I CERTAINLY DIDN'T volunteer to deliver the postcard because I wanted to make new friends in exotic foreign lands. *Au contraire*; I'm a person whose travels are motivated by nature, architecture and food – in other words, all the attractions Barbra Streisand isn't referring to when she natters on about 'peeeeeople who need people'. But there I was on Floreana Island, at the arse-end of the Galapagos, nine hundred kilometres off the coast of Ecuador, and I wanted to send a postcard home to my partner Pamela in Miami. If I expected hand delivery of my own mail, *mano a mano*, it seemed only sporting to pick up somebody else's.

The Floreana post office is really just a raffish wooden barrel plunked down in the middle of the sand, a descendant of one installed in the eighteenth century by whaling crews. In those days it was an optimally efficient system: sailors who were passing through checked the mailbox for letters addressed to their ships' ports of call. Today the barrel is stuffed with postcards from tourists of all nations. You could schlep them home and stamp them, obviously, but the true spirit of the olde mail barrel, according to our guidebook, demands the personal touch.

The day my daughter Miranda and I were in Floreana, most of the mail was addressed to Norwegians and Argentines. But there was one postcard with frolicking sea lions on one side and '*Saluti!*' scrawled on the other, intended for someone named Gina at an *erboristeria*, or herbal pharmacy, in Bassano del Grappa, Italy. I knew this was the home of grappa, the firewater liqueur. I had even been through the town once on a train, so I also knew it was located at the foot of the Alps, in the Veneto region, about 195 kilometres from Venice. Pamela and I had frequent flier tickets to Venice in a few months. I pocketed the card.

Still, I wasn't prepared just to show up cold. When I got back home, I decided to write Gina a letter. I speak a little Italian – that is, I know a lot of hotel and menu words, which I sometimes say in Spanish by mistake. But with the help of a dictionary, I managed to explain all about the mailbox traditions. I assured Gina that there was no social obligation that went along with her receipt of the postcard – although I'd be glad to buy her a beer.

'Mum, you can't send this to strangers,' warned Miranda, who majored in Italian, when I showed her my letter. 'They'll understand you, but they'll think you're a serial killer.'

She rehabilitated my felonious grammar. Off went a letter to Bassano del Grappa. A month later I got an email from someone named Luca. There was a note in Italian, plus a serial-killer English translation that read:

> Dear Sirs VAN GELDER, let off ourself for the postpone what we replay at your letter, but we were outside for a travel. We are very happy to meet yuo in Veneto for make a friendship. If yuo send to as the date of yuor travel we can organise ourself for meeting. Reverence, Gina.

It was around this time that Pamela, who speaks no Italian at all, began asking me pointed questions about exactly how much of our time in Venice was going to be devoted to this project. But I had made a commitment to the spirit of the mailbox, damn it. I sent the dates. Gina/Luca emailed back phone numbers and said we should call when we got to Venice.

A woman answered the phone.

'*Buongiorno*,' I burbled, '*è Gina chi parla?*'

No, it wasn't Gina. It was Edda. Whoever Edda was, she knew exactly who I was – 'You're coming on Monday, yes?' – and we managed, despite my rotten Italian, to communicate some particulars about the railway schedules. 'Just go to the counter in the station,' she instructed.

When I got off the phone, I realised that I had no clue about which counter she meant. The ticket booth? The postcard had been addressed to a pharmacy. Could it be in the train station? Did it have a counter? A few hours later I called again, and this time a male voice answered. No, Gina wasn't there. Neither was Edda. The male voice belonged to Luca, my email buddy, who explained to me in halting English that the train station was not very big and I shouldn't worry. Then he added, 'You perhaps don't know that Gina really doesn't speak any English? As you will see when you meet her on Monday.'

I was beginning to doubt her existence altogether. Was Gina actually a dog, the mascot of the pharmacy? Was I the butt of a joke that had already travelled seven thousand kilometres?

'You really don't have to come if you don't want to,' I told Pamela. No, no, she'd come. But we just wouldn't stay any longer than we had to.

Our doubts began to melt the second we got off the train. There, carrying a single red rose and a big sign that said 'Welcome Lindsy to Bassano del Grappa', were a college-aged guy and two grinning sixtyish ladies. One of them – an Italian leprechaun – immediately grabbed me in a bear hug. The more bashful of the two, dressed in brown and wearing glasses, turned out to be Gina. My new best friend was her sister Edda, dolled up in bright red and wearing major eye make-up. The guy was Luca, their younger sister's son, an engineering student who, alone among the group, had once studied English. He had his dictionary out. So did I.

Before I could proffer the small piece of cardboard that had gathered us together in this spot, Pamela and I were whisked off to a restaurant for lunch. It was like being plopped down on the set of *Amarcord*: we were joined by Luca's mother, who tooled in on a bicycle, and briefly by his father, as well as a parade of cooks and waiters to whom we were introduced as The Girls from America Who Brought the Postcard. Mounds of antipasto arrived at the table, followed by enormous platters of pasta with lobster and heaps of delicate baby greens. Prosecco, the champagne of the Veneto, flowed like the Brenta. And a good thing, too, since most of the conversation that we could all muster had to do with the cuisine of the region. Someone would proclaim '*sardele in saor*', and the rest of the group would 'mmmm' and 'ahhhh', and then someone else would chime in with *spaghetti vongole* or *radicchio alla griglia*, followed by more orgasmic choruses. From time to time one of us would raise a glass and toast, 'From the Galapagos to Bassano del

Grappa!' and we would all whoop. I noticed that Pamela was not looking at her watch. The family's *erboristeria* was currently closed for renovations, we learned, and perhaps they all had some time on their hands. But that alone didn't really explain the brass-band welcome. Nor did the famous postcard, which I finally presented to Gina over sorbet laced with a lethal dollop of grappa. She glanced at it, remarked that it was from a customer and packed it away in her purse, not to be referred to again. The postcard was merely the message. Making friendship was the medium.

And what was a little translation technicality among friends? By the time the cheque was paid – the family refused to take our crumpled lire notes – we were all feeling punchily pleased with our ability to leapfrog the language barrier. A tour of the town was proposed. Bassano is actually a gem of a place, with a spectacular Palladian wooden bridge spanning the Brenta River and a sinister castle on its banks – the home, Luca explained, of Ezzolino da Roma, a bloodthirsty tyrant so infamous that he was cited in Dante's *Inferno*. Then we strolled on a bluff above the river past a row of lollipop-like trees. Bassano was notoriously active in the Resistance, Gina told us, and in 1944 the German army hanged thirty-one of the town's young men in retaliation – one for each tree. 'I wrote a poem about it once,' Gina added shyly. How nice, I thought, with the genteel condescension of the professional journalist, a pharmacist who expresses herself in poetry. We tramped around to churches, Roman ruins, even a museum of grappa, where Gina insisted on buying us not one but three bottles of the stuff – regular, honey and blueberry – as souvenirs

Certainly we would also like to see a little of the region? *Si, si, certo.* Into the family station wagon we piled, Luca trying to drive and riffle through the dictionary at the same time. By then, we more or less had our schtick down. The Italians spoke slowly, with infinite patience and maximum hand-jive. Dictionary pages flipped like decks of cards. Somehow we managed to progress beyond cuisine to pets, gambling, art, birth order, the weather in Miami, the allure of Venice, Edda's arthritis, my bad knee, our feelings about spirituality versus organised religion, even politics and politicians (for that one we all used the international sign of stuffing one's finger down one's throat). We took pictures of each other in the main square of Marostica, where the residents dress up as bishops and queens every autumn and enact a days-long chess game. We climbed to the fort above the town. By then it was getting dark, and, alas, we had a train to catch.

But it was decided that we would first meet the family cats and dogs. At Gina and Edda's house we got another surprise. Gina had written poetry all right – she brought us out copies of all her books, as well as a CD on which several of her verses had been set to modern classical music and sung by the soprano Isabella Frati. These, she insisted, were gifts: one set for us and one for Miranda.

By now we were sagging under the weight of three bottles of grappa and a small library of books, plus the CDs and a multilingual guidebook to Marostica that Gina had impulsively bought after Luca and I had exhausted our duelling dictionaries in the search for words to describe chess pieces and military architecture – all in exchange for one lousy postcard. Nor would the sisters dream of letting us take the train back to Venice. They drove us all the way to Piazzale Roma, the last niblet of mainland before one has to switch to a waterbus or gondola. We kissed, cried, offered our respective spare rooms any time, promised to be fluent in each other's language the next time we met.

And indeed, with the help of my dog-eared dictionary, I am slowly reading Gina's poetry. The one about the thirty-one martyrs is a favourite, but there are also sexy, smouldering love poems. Pamela has been stockpiling South Florida culinary goodies to send the ladies. Luca and I have become email pen pals. I correct his English, he corrects my Italian and tells me what the family is up to. Edda was recently in Australia. Somehow I feel certain she made herself understood.

Meanwhile, the postcard I mailed home to Pamela from Floreana hasn't turned up yet. I find myself getting oddly excited at the idea of meeting whichever stranger, speaking whatever language, eventually shows up with it. I may have been the one who went to the Galapagos. But it was Gina and her family who taught me about real adventure travel.

Brief Encounter

CAROLYN SWINDELL

'Carolyn is far too interested in the affairs of children around her.' So said Carolyn Swindell's year two report card – and no one who knows her has ever tried to dispute that assertion. After graduating with a degree in Japanese, she lived in Japan for one crazy year and turned her hand to spin-doctoring in the world of Australian politics. Three years in the Northern Territory convinced her that she is not the next Crocodile Dundee after all and she now lives in Canberra, working in rugby union to finance her expensive travel and postgraduate study habits. She occasionally turns her hand to freelance writing, obviously thinking that other children are just as interested in her affairs now. She thinks that perfection is a five-day cricket match.

DECENT UNDERWEAR – it's important.

There's nothing like humping your life around on your back for months and having the freedom to go wherever you want, but some days the shine of the traveller's life is not so obvious. You want to see some familiar faces and have just one transaction be straightforward. Generally these moods pass quickly, but sometimes when your spirits have been eroded by the unparalleled joys of third world travel, you just need a clean pair of knickers and a good cup of tea. And since you can't always rely on getting a proper cup of tea, decent underwear is critical.

I anticipated this when packing; I had ample practical but attractive underwear to see me safely on my travels. I sacrificed valuable backpack space to include five pairs of white cotton briefs – not saucy man-killers, but not too shabby if there ever was call for an inspection. They were comfortable without being nanna knickers: the quintessential backpacker underpants.

These knickers served me well through countless handwashes in hostel basins and overnight dryings on improvised clotheslines. They didn't ride up when I walked or pinch when I sat for hours on trains. Yes, they served me well. But all good things must come to an end.

I arrived in Buenos Aires and, after months of frugality on the road, decided to treat myself to an actual hotel: a four-star room of my own, with a bath no less, and all a mere spitting distance from where my well-thumbed Lonely Planet told me the action would be. No need for my sleeping bag here; I had a real bed, topped with a mountain of pillows. But all that was to be enjoyed later.

I showered, and savoured the novelty of unpacking the entire contents of my backpack, even hanging some clothes up. Then, feeling refreshed, I strode out to face the world.

Before I went to Argentina, I knew a lot about Buenos Aires, all my knowledge gained from watching Madonna sashay about in *Evita*. I knew that a young Eva Duarte had found the capital terribly exciting when she arrived from the country, and I knew that all the men of the city were very sexy and could tango from the day they could walk.

Still feeling wealthy and self-indulgent, I jumped into a taxi and hesitantly rattled off '*Feria de San Telmo, por favor.*' I was pleased when the cabbie appeared to know what I was talking about.

Immediately after congratulating myself for completing this great linguistic feat, I was filled with self-doubt. What if Feria de San Telmo actually meant 'shallow grave' or something similar instead of the intended flea markets in the suburb of San Telmo? I began urgently riffling through my guidebook, trying to estab-lish if we were headed in the right direction. All I achieved was to make myself feel carsick, because a few minutes later we pulled up about a block from Feria de San Telmo.

The market was full of antiques and knick-knacks. Local artists displayed their paintings and sculptures, many of which were really quite good despite being so obviously pitched at the tourists. After a little wandering, I elbowed my way to the front of a crowd that had assembled to watch a tango extravaganza. I ended up watching the spectacle for what seemed like hours, admiring the grace of the moves and the sheer sensuality of the dance. I thought my attraction to men in trilby hats had ended when Wham! broke up in the 1980s. Apparently not.

Still, the longer I watched, the less I saw the men. The troupe was made up of four men and one woman who danced with each of them in turn. She was amazing; you would never see anyone like her at home.

If you looked closely, you'd notice that her black dress was probably twenty years old – a worn satin in a style that hadn't been fashionable for a long time. It was not so black any more either and the fabric was wearing slightly thin in places. But you wouldn't look closely. You'd never notice that the dress looked tired, you'd be too wrapped up in the dance. You'd throw this dress out if you found it in the back of your wardrobe – a ruffled reminder of styles you had loved as a kid that now made you cringe – and yet, watching her move so sensually in the arms of her partner, you'd covet this dress for all it represented.

The black satin was taut against her slightly large bottom and the dress was split almost to her hip, revealing one shapely, toned leg. Not toned from hours at the gym, not toned like an athlete's, toned like that of a woman who danced the tango late into every evening.

I longed for legs like hers. I could not imagine a shape more womanly.

The show ended and the dancers moved around the circle collecting money from the assembled crowd. I threw some US dollars into the proffered trilby. It would have been more if she had passed by. I was no longer so interested in the tango of the men, now I wanted to master the dance myself, to be as much of a woman as she was.

The crowd dispersed and the dancers moved together, smoking cigarettes and chatting casually.

To those of us who aren't good at much of anything, people who are very good at something seem entirely at ease with others who are good at the same thing. The dancers seemed just as purposeful in their movements as they smoked their cigarettes and changed their shoes as they did while dancing.

This was very intimidating, but I longed to speak to her – to find out, with my almost non-existent Spanish, how long she'd been dancing the tango, and whether there was any hope for someone like me who had only today discovered the tango that beat wildly within me.

I steeled myself. This was like approaching the cool gang at high school and addressing one of them in front of all of the others. I refused to let this flashback to my teenage years stop me; I desperately wanted to talk tango turkey with the satin-clad dancer.

I was merely centimetres away from her when something caught my eye. I turned and looked in the window of the shop next to me. Or rather, I looked at the window. What I saw horrified me.

I saw me. And far from being the sensuous temptress I now fancied myself as, I saw myself as others would have seen me, as my mother would have seen me. My hair was pulled back into a ponytail; well, some was, the rest hung limply or stuck out at angles usually associated with electrocution in cartoons. I smoothed my hair as I self-consciously examined myself in the window. My T-shirt was misshapen and stained, my jeans weren't clean. Even my Dunlop Volleys had lost some of their appeal.

All dreams I had of dancing the tango were lost as I focussed on my appearance. I couldn't talk to the dancers now. More than a decade after high school had finished, on a totally different continent, I could still find a cool gang to make myself feel inadequate.

My shoulders slumped and I walked away along the wide streets leading back to Microcentro. Buenos Aires is the perfect city for a walker and ordinarily I loved a walk. But this one was torturous.

Everywhere I looked I saw beautiful young Argentinean couples walking arm in arm. He was always incredibly handsome. Always. Every man in Buenos Aires seemed to look like Antonio Banderas. And what united the young women was their confidence. It seeped out of every pore; it screamed *woman* and every Antonio lapped it up. Bottoms of various sizes were squeezed into tight Capri pants and miniskirts. These women rolled their hips as they walked like Gina Lollabridgida in their high heels.

And they all had VPLs. The Visible Panty Line was everywhere.

Ordinarily this would make me feel better. I would feel superior somehow because I *never* have a VPL. I would tell myself that I am too classy for that. Today, though, it just made me feel worse. I felt androgynous, as though I had thrown away my gender when I picked up my backpack.

Lost in thought, I missed the turn-off for my hotel and found myself in Boulevard Florida. The joint was jumping. It was after nine o'clock and things were just starting to warm up. All around me more young Argentinean couples were enjoying each other's company.

I looked at myself in the window of another shop. Still shocking. As I examined my reflection, though, there was a transformation in what I saw. It was like one of those Magic Eye pictures where you look at something long enough to see something altogether different. I started to see a different me.

Beyond my reflection was a dress. It wasn't much – a simple black dress with a V neck – but I knew I would carry it, and it would carry me, through the rest of my travels.

I raced in, grabbed the dress off the rack and made for the changing rooms, striding purposefully through the enormous shop and holding the dress high.

Ladies' changing rooms are like McDonald's – when you enter one, you could be anywhere on the planet; they are all exactly the same. I pulled the dress over my head and faced the mirror. It was great.

The music in the shop was truly terrible, a fact they tried to mask by playing it far too loud. I was keen to get out as soon as I could hand my credit card over, so I pulled the dress off quickly. The annoying pop song had actually made its way into my brain and I was singing along with the chorus as I reached down to pick up my jeans from the floor.

I stood in the changing room, holding my jeans, and studied my reflection. Again I didn't like what I saw.

I hadn't put on much weight; I looked pretty good despite not having been to the gym in months. Walking all day will do that. So it wasn't that. It was my underwear. My trusty traveller's knickers were no longer white, they were grey. The appeal they'd had when I bought them, the multipurpose practicality and attractiveness, was gone; now they were simply practical. If I was honest, they were pretty much on their last legs in the practicality stakes too – the elastic was shot.

It was time to farewell my quintessential backpacker underwear and invest in some new, untested brands. Risky, but necessary.

Emerging from the changing room I was again assaulted by pop torture. Evidently there was wave upon wave of this appalling music lying in wait for me, so I needed to find the underwear and get out of there as fast as I could.

A sales assistant approached me and spoke rapidly in Spanish. She was very fashionably dressed but looked to be older than my mother. I wondered how she could stand to work with that music; it would drive me insane, let alone my mother.

'*No hablo español*,' I mumbled with an apologetic shrug.

She smiled at me and pointed to the dress. 'You buy?' she asked.

'*Si*,' I said, trying to work out how to tell her I wanted to look around first. I pointed at myself and circled my finger like I was stirring a cup of tea with it.

'*Si, si*,' she smiled. She grabbed the dress and pointed to a cash register at the front of the shop. Then she pointed at herself and said 'Carolina.'

I smiled. '*Si. Gracias*, Carolina.' Apart from the brief exchange with the taxi driver, she was the first person I had spoken to all day and I felt like I had made a new friend. I almost wished she would come shopping with me.

All the colours of the rainbow were represented in the lingerie section, as well as many colours not seen anywhere in nature. There were patterns and prints and many tiny, tiny knickers with matching bras. The Argentineans seemed to take the term 'brief' literally; it was almost not worth wearing these knickers, there was so little to them. I began to wonder if the extreme bikini wax might have been named after the wrong South American country.

Two songs later I finally found something suitable, hidden right at the back. No wonder the Argentinean girls all had VPLs – it was nearly impossible to buy anything that would seem to fit an even slightly rounded bottom. I grabbed three pairs of suitable white cotton underpants of the kind I favoured and headed back to Carolina at the front of the store.

Carolina greeted me like an old friend and chattered away in Spanish, perhaps thinking I had somehow mastered the Spanish language while in the lingerie department. She folded the dress and wrapped it in tissue paper and then reached across for the underpants.

She picked them up and examined them, distaste clear on her face. She pointed at the underpants and then at me, obviously questioning whether they were for me. I nodded.

Carolina shook her head and put the underpants down. 'No.'

'*Si*,' I said.

Carolina shook her head again, this time more emphatically. 'No.'

I nodded my head, also more emphatically. '*Si*.' Then I added '*Gracias*' in the hope it would end this interaction that was rapidly changing my view of my new friend Carolina.

Carolina threw the underpants down on the counter in disgust and folded her arms across her chest. 'No,' this time with even more vehemence. She clearly did not wish for me to buy these underpants.

I began to get cross. I may not be as glamourous as the Argentinean girls, but I had money and could use it however I pleased. And right now, buying those underpants was how I bloody well pleased. I pulled my credit card out of my wallet and slid it across the counter with the underpants.

'*Si*,' I said firmly through clenched teeth, wishing I knew how to ask to speak to the manager in Spanish.

Carolina handed me my credit card and motioned for me to wait. If I hadn't wanted the black dress so much, I would have taken the opportunity to run away, but I waited. I tried to catch the eye of another sales assistant to see if I could escape the clutches of crazy Carolina. No one paid any attention to me. I knew that they worked on commission, so once Carolina had told me her name, none of the others would bother; I was Carolina's baby now.

She bustled back a moment or two later, still chattering madly at me in Spanish. She handed me the smallest pair of underpants I have ever seen, nodding with satisfaction.

'Better for you,' she said, smiling broadly and nodding.

It was hard for me not to laugh. I was amused at how little there was to these knickers; they were light years from my practical-but-attractives. But I was also kind of annoyed that Carolina was so clearly trying to work her commission by pressuring me into buying much more expensive underwear than I needed.

She must have thought I was stupid. I looked at Carolina and she was smiling and nodding. I picked up the underpants and tried to be polite and look as though I was seriously considering her ridiculous suggestion.

Out of curiosity, I looked at the price. They were much cheaper than the ones I had selected for myself. I looked at Carolina and she was still smiling broadly.

'*No, gracias,*' I said, sliding the tiny knickers across the counter and putting my practical-but-attractives back on top of the folded dress. I smiled as nicely as I could, feeling a little bad that I had misjudged her.

'Better for you,' she said again and pushed them back across the counter at me.

'*No, gracias,*' I said again, this time more firmly, and handed her the pile with my black dress and practical-but-attractives.

Carolina crossed her arms and shook her head, violently this time.

A standoff.

A long pause.

Eventually Carolina exhaled sharply and said, 'Okay.' I thought I had won.

'Together,' she said, motioning for me to follow her.

For the next fifteen minutes, Carolina and I wandered around the lingerie section, trying to reach a compromise. Carolina was determined I would buy some of the Argentinean skimpy knickers and I was determined to buy something as close to my old trusty travel knickers as I could find.

Compromise was reached by millimetres. Eventually we found a pair we were both happy with. Carolina smiled at me with victory in her eyes before grabbing three pairs and rushing back to the register.

I pulled my credit card out again and finally the transaction was complete. As Carolina handed me the bag containing my purchases, she once again surprised me.

She pointed at me. 'You beautiful girl; don't forgot.'

The English was flawed but the sentiment was obvious, and I was genuinely speechless.

As I walked away I realised what she'd done. Carolina had gone out of her way and done herself out of some commission just to put the tango back into a strange girl's step. That day, thanks to her stubbornness, I switched from practical-but-attractive to pure tango, and not just in my underwear. I've never switched back, either.

That evening, I walked along Boulevard Florida, no VPL but a lot of Argentinean confidence in my rolling hips. The Eva Duarte within was back.

Damascus by Teatime

DON MEREDITH

Don Meredith's travel essays have appeared in *Poets and Writers*, *Image*, Salon.com, the *San Francisco Examiner* and the *Texas Review*. He lives on Lamu Island, Kenya, and writes for *Travel News*, based in Nairobi. His most recent book is *Where the Tigers Were: Travels through Literary Landscapes*, and he is completing *Varieties of Darkness: The World of 'The English Patient'*.

'YOUR MISTER T.S. ELIOT, please, in what poem does he ask many questions?'

'Questions?'

'You must know Mister T.S. Eliot?'

'Yes, of course. Questions. "The Love Song of J. Alfred Prufrock" do you mean? "Shall I part my hair behind? Do I dare to eat a peach?" That what you have in mind?'

'Yes, Mister Alfred Prufrock is the one. But Ernest Hemingway? How could the man who wrote *The Old Man and the Sea*, the story of a person's struggle against great odds, commit suicide? It seems your writers invent one thing and live something else.'

I had been warned of strangers lurking on Syrian street corners. But lost as I am in the heart of Deraa – tired, ravenous, alone – Abdullah Hassan Abud is more than I could have bargained for.

A high school English teacher in his early thirties, with pale eyes and clipped hair, he wears the stubble beard that's *de rigueur* for young Syrian men. 'May I be of assistance?' he asks. 'You are lost? I will direct you somewhere.'

Abdullah tours me through Deraa's dowdy streets and proudly shows off its three equally shabby hotels. I choose the al-Salam for no better reason than it's the last I've seen and I won't have to traipse back to the others. Next Abdullah treats me to Nescafé and condensed milk, a Syrian cappuccino, at an open-air café in the town square.

In the funk of late afternoon, after a hard day's travel to this market town on the flank of the southern Hauran, I fail to take Abdullah up on the subject of Hemingway's self-destruction. Undismayed, he pursues his hypothesis: writers create one thing, live another. 'Take Lawrence, for example.'

'D.H. Lawrence? Lawrence Durrell?'

'Colonel Lawrence – the one you call, for reasons I do not understand, Lawrence of Arabia. What about him? Did he not know that when the Turks were beaten, the British and French would divide Arabia as if it were theirs to divide?'

'He didn't know.'

'You're sure?'

'The Sykes-Picot Treaty established English and French hegemony in the Middle East. It was kept a secret until the war's end. Lawrence knew nothing of it. Nonetheless, he suspected Britain's motives and urged the Arabs to rush into Damascus ahead of the English troops. The Arabs would then be seen as victors who'd earned the right to govern themselves.'

'Did he really believe they would?'

'Hoped – but no, he didn't truly believe. It was a deep problem for him – part of his self-hatred – deceiving the Arabs so they'd follow him and help the English win the war.'

'Forgive me, please, but I believe I do not like the English so much.'

After a restless night at the al-Salam, I stumble out early and head for the railway station in the middle of town. I've bussed to Deraa, but hope to train to Damascus on the old Hejaz Railway that Lawrence risked so much dynamite and time blowing up. The station is two stories of painted brick with peaked roofs and an odd assortment of picturesque chimneys. A brass bell, green with age, and an old-fashioned clock cling like limpets to the crumbling wall outside the stationmaster's office. Three dozen wooden freight cars string through the marshalling yards. Wild flowers blossom between the rails. A pair of women in violet kaftans squat outside the waiting room, nursing babies. A rusty sign swings above an open door: 'Information'.

Inside, a little man in a large visored cap, possibly a hand-me-down from a Luftwaffe officer, peers over a high counter. 'May I be of help, sir?' he asks in clipped English.

'A train to Damascus – is such a thing possible?'

'One train each week, and today, dear friend, today is the day. Noon. Four hours to Damascus. You will arrive at teatime.'

'May I purchase a ticket?'

'Ticket? Ticket? Dear friend, is still early. Plenty time for ticket.'

In Lawrence's day, government offices faced the town square. Now nondescript buildings painted in mind-numbing pastels border the drab quadrangle. At its heart, guarded by triple swags of heavy chain, stands a fountain of monstrous modernity in which a few gallons of swamp water steep beneath primordial scum. On its sad perimeter, ragged shoeshine boys scuttle after clients, and adolescent girls beg coins.

'Young boys shining the shoes, they are Kurds,' Abdullah says, dropping into a chair at the outdoor café as if knowing instinctively I would be here.

'How do you know, Abdullah?'

'They are speaking Kurdish language, but I cannot understand what they say.'

A trio of girls sidles up to our table with outstretched hands. Their dark flowing hair cascades over the tiers of their neon-coloured frocks: chrome yellow, scalding pink, effervescent violet. 'And these?' I ask, reaching for a coin.

'Gypsies.' Abdullah shakes his head in warning. 'Give them nothing. Be watchful. They steal everything.'

The girls move in, whining, wheedling, reaching for my pockets. I press coins into a small hand but they're thrust back. Not enough. More. Money. Real money. The smallest and bravest grabs at my camera. Before she can wrap her fingers around it, the waiter gives her a crack on the head with his knuckles. She drops dramatically, then drags herself away, howling.

'Is Deraa always like this?' I ask Abdullah, thinking of Lawrence's capture and torture at the hands of Deraa's Turkish commandant.

Abdullah blinks with incomprehension. 'Why not? I have lived here all my life. It has always been this way.' Then, catching his breath, he begins a rapid string of disconnected inquiries he must have lain awake half the night working out. They are not really questions, for he doesn't expect answers, but in a burst he asserts that it is inconceivable there is anyone who doesn't believe in God; that reckless sex is rapidly destroying Western civilisation; that every member of the United States Congress is Jewish.

'How else can you explain America's Middle East policy?'

His misconceptions of the West mirror my own unclear notions of Islam and Arabs. To show that I know *something* of his country, I ask about Syrian support for Iran in the Iran-Iraq war. 'Isn't it true that Iran still gives Syria two thousand barrels of free oil a day for providing that support?'

Abdullah glances nervously around. Talking Syrian politics is not a popular Syrian pastime. He leans nearer, whispering, 'These things we must not know. They are military secrets. Please, speak of something else.'

So much we can't say. Yet, lingering over coffee in the mid-morning sun, we share the feeling that for now none of it matters. Finding me lost on a street corner, Abdullah possibly saved me a night in the open. He's treated me to coffees, shown me the town, and out of this, a friendship has evolved. If we can't talk politics, we can at least speak of the bill. Who will pay? I press money into the waiter's hand. Abdullah snatches it back. 'This is not possible,' he says sharply. 'You are guest in my country.'

'Abdullah, you've paid for *everything*.'

'It is as it must be.'

The waiter understands. Only Abdullah's money is acceptable. This generous, hard-working young teacher again pays our bill, then takes my arm and leads me toward the station.

'Abdullah, what about teaching your classes? You're already late for school.'

'It is arranged. A colleague will look after the students so that I may see you off to Damascus.'

When we reach the station, the train crew, a trio in checked keffiyehs, sprawls on a meadow of spring grass between the rails. It's minutes before our scheduled departure, but there's no train and no one's in a hurry. Abdullah vanishes and, a moment later, reappears with a chair he carefully arranges in the shade. 'Sit, please. You must rest before your journey.' No arguments allowed. I sit. The women in the violet kaftans move onto the platform, nursing their babies. A man in a suit and tie clutches an attaché case and paces nervously beside an ancient couple lugging cardboard boxes bound with string. The little man in the Luftwaffe cap glances at the antique clock. It's 3.23 – just as it was at 7 a.m.

'Ticket? Ticket?' he shouts cheerfully when I offer him a wad of Syrian pounds. 'Plenty time for ticket.'

Finally the train arrives, rumbling through the marketplace, scattering chickens, fruit vendors and old men on bicycles before it slides into the marshalling yards, a sleek pumpkin-coloured Jordan Railways diesel drawing a caboose and a pair of antique wooden passenger carriages.

'Good-looking train,' I tell Abdullah, who has grown silent as my departure nears.

'Is Jordan Railways and must be sent back. Syrian train will carry you to Damascus.'

The diesel is uncoupled, shunted, sent solo back to Amman. Then, just as Abdullah said, a Syrian Railways engine is nursed, coughing dryly, out of a locomotive shed. The crew couples it to the antique cars and the man in the Luftwaffe cap issues me a cardboard ticket – Deraa–Damascus – then punches it briskly with a toy conductor's punch.

At the bottom of the steps leading to the third-class carriage, Abdullah clutches me, kisses me on both cheeks. *'Ma'a salaama*, my friend.' He wipes his eyes with the back of a hand. 'You will write to me soon. I await your letter. You will explain all things about Mister Hemingway.'

Before I can reply, he presses a small, carefully wrapped package of food into my hands and is gone, bursting across the marshalling yards to lose himself in the shadowy station.

I pass along grim rows of slat seats in the vacant third-class carriage, then cross the open vestibule to first class. After stowing my bag in a seedy compartment, I settle into a threadbare seat. The train lurches forward. Through the smudged window, in a street beyond the station, I see Abdullah standing stolidly in the sunlight, watching the train begin its journey. He raises a hand in farewell. He isn't smiling.

My Beirut Hostage Crisis

ROLF POTTS

Rolf Potts is the author of *Vagabonding: An Uncommon Guide to the Art of Long-Term World Travel*. He has written travel stories for Salon.com, *Condé Nast Traveler*, *National Geographic Traveler* and National Public Radio, and his work has been reprinted in several anthologies, including *The Best American Travel Writing 2000*. Rolf keeps no permanent address, but feels somewhat at home in Thailand, Korea, Egypt, Oregon and Kansas. His virtual home is www.rolfpotts.com. His second book, *Marco Polo Didn't Go There*, will be published in late 2004.

I FIRST MET MR IBRAHIM in the Hamra district of West Beirut. At the time, I'd been searching for a pub that had been recommended to me second-hand, and I wasn't having much luck. I was studying my street map on the corner of rues Hamra and Jeanne d'Arc when Mr Ibrahim approached me, looking innocuous in his blue jeans, plaid shirt and neatly trimmed goatee.

'Are you lost?' he asked me.

'Not really,' I said. 'I know where I am; I just can't find the place I want to go.'

'I am Mr Ibrahim,' he said, gesturing grandly at the buildings of Beirut, 'and this is my city.' He looked to be in his early thirties, but he spoke like he thought of himself as a wizened old patriarch. 'Where do you wish to go?'

'Well, it's a pub that a friend of a friend told me about, but I'm not sure if you would know where . . .'

'This is my city!' Mr Ibrahim bellowed happily, giving me a start. He grinned intensely as I attempted to continue.

'Oh, right. Well, I'm looking for a . . .'

'Where are you from?'

'I'm from America.'

'America!' Mr Ibrahim yelled, his voice echoing through the street. Still grinning, he pulled out his wallet and produced a dollar bill. 'What is this?' he asked me.

'Um, it's a dollar.'

'And what does it say?'

'It says, "One dollar."'

'No!' Mr Ibrahim boomed. He held the dollar up in front of my face. 'It says, "In . . . God . . .we . . . trust!"'

'In God we trust,' I repeated, not sure what the point was.

'That's why your country is great: because you trust in God.' Mr Ibrahim magnanimously handed me the dollar bill. 'You keep this,' he said.

'Well, that's nice,' I said holding the dollar back out to him, 'but I don't need a dollar as much as I need to find . . .'

'You keep this!' Mr Ibrahim hollered happily, snatching the

dollar from my hand and stuffing it into my shirt pocket. 'Every day you must pray to God for sex, and he will give you more dollars than you ever dreamed of.'

'Pray for sex?'

'Yes, pray for sexus!' He beamed proudly, as if he'd just changed my life.

'Oh,' I said, catching his accent. 'Pray for success.'

'Sex-cess!' Mr Ibrahim yelled, suddenly looking impatient. 'Where do you want to go? This is my city, and I can show you anywhere.'

'Well, a friend's friend told me about a pub called the Hole in the Wall . . .' I began. As I spoke, Mr Ibrahim pulled out his cellphone and began to furiously punch in numbers. '. . . I'm just not sure if I'm even in the right . . .'

I paused as Mr Ibrahim began to shout Arabic into his cellphone. He stopped for a moment and looked over at me. 'Where do we go?'

'The Hole in the Wall.'

'The Holy Diwah!' he yelled at his phone. He punched another button and put the phone back into his pocket.

'Who was that you were talking to?' I asked.

'It's okay; we will take you there. It is my pleasure.'

'Yes, but who's we? Who was on the phone?'

'That was Abdul.'

'Is he a friend of yours?'

'Of course not!' Mr Ibrahim boomed, laughing. 'Abdul is my bodyguard!'

Five minutes later, a massive young man drove up in a gold Mercedes E300. The door locks, I noticed, were tipped with rhinestones. At Mr Ibrahim's grand insistence, I took the shotgun seat, and – for all practical purposes – I was his hostage for the next three days.

The hours before my first encounter with Mr Ibrahim stand out in vivid contrast with what was to follow, if nothing else, for their relative peace and coherence.

I'd arrived in Beirut the previous afternoon, but I hadn't set off to explore the city itself until that morning. Striking out from my hotel, I strolled past the impressively redeveloped central business district, the Roman ruins of Cardo Maximus and the idyllic campus of the American University.

The most intriguing thing I discovered that morning, however, was the stark evidence of the civil war that had once raged through the city. An abundance of bullet-scarred buildings stood in bleak contrast to the ongoing renovations, particularly along the Green Line that once separated Muslim West Beirut from the Christian East.

I'm not sure why these war remnants proved so fascinating for me. In a way, I don't even like war tourism, as it reduces certain places – Sarajevo, Belfast, Phnom Penh – into dull, de facto thrill destinations, relevant only for the visceral buzz of recent history. Here, travellers photograph soldiers and barbed wire with the same blind compulsion that inspires them to photograph the Eiffel Tower in Paris.

In Beirut, which has been open to American travellers since only 1997, I found it difficult not to be a war tourist. The battered buildings of the old buffer zone proved a grim reminder of not just the Muslim-Christian discord that symbolised the war, but the international factors that started and prolonged it: French favouritism, American geopolitics, Syrian opportunism, Israeli brutality, Iranian radicalism, Palestinian rage. In some places, bullet holes in buildings were so common that they seemed a part of the architecture – a congenital concrete defect that just happened to afflict that neighbourhood.

By its very definition, war tourism is a fickle activity. Stunned as I was by the evidence of war, sobered as I was by its devastation, I left the Green Line that evening looking for a place to party.

Using directions copied from a month-old email, I began to walk in search of the Hole in the Wall pub. Less than an hour later, I found myself in the ruthlessly gung-ho custody of a man who called himself Mr Ibrahim.

When I first got into Mr Ibrahim's Mercedes, I thought maybe he was one of those rich guys who run with showgirls and compulsively hand out boxes of Cuban cigars and bottles of Hennessy. As it turned out, he was a celibate teetotaller who vetoed our trip to the Hole in the Wall the moment I mentioned that the place served alcohol.

We ended up driving to the Weekland, an upscale buffet restaurant that had been booked up that night for a Sunni Muslim wedding. Unfazed by our lack of a reservation, Mr Ibrahim bullied his way into getting us a table overlooking the courtyard fountain. As Mr Ibrahim instructed Abdul the Bodyguard to fill my plate with lamb, *kibbe* and hummus from the buffet, I took in my surroundings. Down in the courtyard, an immaculately dressed bride and groom cut their cake and posed for a photographer. Across the restaurant, groups of relatives watched this unfold live on a big-screen TV. At the tables around us, tuxedo-clad Sunni men smoked cigarettes and squinted at their cellphones. The Sunni women chatted amongst themselves, looking refined and downright sexy in their designer dresses and silken headscarves.

The Lebanese food was fantastic, and Mr Ibrahim was thrilled that I ate it with such enthusiasm.

'Do you like my food?' he asked me, grinning like a madman.

'It's great,' I said between mouthfuls.

'How about my city? Did you see my city today?'

'Yes, I walked around some this afternoon.'

'What did you see? Did you see the Hard Rock Cafe?'

'No, but I visited the American Univ –'

'That was a trick question: Beirut has two Hard Rock Cafes!'

'Wow. Well, I haven't seen either one of them yet, but –'

'Two Hard Rock Cafes!' Mr Ibrahim hollered happily.

'Right, but today I walked along the old Green Line and . . .'

'I'm sorry, where did you say?'

'The Green Line. I went walking . . .'

'The Green Line is not for tourists!' Mr Ibrahim yelled, shaking his finger at me. For the first time since I'd met him, Mr Ibrahim was not grinning, and this gave me a chill.

'What?' I stammered.

'The Green Line has only bullets and old buildings. Why do you want to see that?'

'Well, I thought it would be interesting to . . .'

'Do these people look like terrorists?' Mr Ibrahim gestured angrily at the wedding guests, his voice echoing off the walls.

'Of course they don't look like terrorists.'

'Of course not! Look at them! This is like Europe. Does this not look like Europe?'

'Yes, it's very nice.'

'Then why do you go to look at buildings with bullets?'

'I don't know. I guess it just seemed . . .'

'There were 180 Lebanese on the *Titanic*!'

I stared at Mr Ibrahim, momentarily speechless. Since it looked like his grin might return, I decided to play along. 'Really?' I said, completely oblivious to how this factoid could have any relevance. 'One hundred and eighty Lebanese were on the *Titanic*?'

'Of course! They were all rich men, businessmen. Like Europeans. Do you think they would let terrorists onto the *Titanic*?'

'I'd imagine they wouldn't.'

'Of course not! The Lebanese have always been rich people. Important people. Do you know how many Lebanese there are in Bill Clinton's cabinet?'

'I don't know.'

'Four! There are four Lebanese in Bill Clinton's cabinet. I know this, and I am not even American! And the president of Ecuador. Do you know where he is from?'

'Well, I'd imagine he's from Ecuador.'

'He is from Lebanon!' Mr Ibrahim roared, obviously having a good time again. 'And when Boris Yeltsin needed surgery for his heart, where do you think his surgeon was from?'

'Lebanon?'

Mr Ibrahim beamed at me. 'I think you are a genius. The

103

surgeon was from Lebanon. He could have had any surgeon in the world, but he wanted the best, and the best was from Lebanon.'

Mr Ibrahim went on like this nonstop for twenty minutes. Once he had exhausted the topic of Lebanese pride, he went on to rant about the evils of tobacco and alcohol, the virtues of America, the scourge of foreign labourers in Lebanon, and how Syrians smell like pigs and dogs. The whole time this was going on, Abdul the Bodyguard blissfully ignored his boss, shovelling down plate after plate of the buffet food. Whenever Mr Ibrahim would leave the table to get more food or bully the wait staff, Adbul would smile mischievously and point out cute girls in the wedding party.

Later, when Abdul was driving us back to my hotel, Mr Ibrahim laid out our plans for the next day. 'Tomorrow, we will go to Byblos,' he said. 'I will show you Lebanon, and you can teach me English. How is my English? Is it bad?' Mr Ibrahim grinned at me from the back seat, obviously fishing for a compliment.

I decided to shoot him straight. 'Well, your vocabulary is good, but your . . .'

'I took many lessons from an institute near the American University.'

'Yes, well your pronunciation could . . .'

'I speak English like an American, yes?' Mr Ibrahim shouted. He grinned, ebullient, in the back seat.

'Well, kind of. But your pronunciation could use some work.'

Mr Ibrahim looked concerned for just a fraction of a second. 'You must teach me to make it better. We will be business partners: I will show you Lebanon, and you will teach me English.'

'Okay, well the best way to improve your pronunciation is to –'

'I think you are the best teacher, so I will be the best tour guide!'

'. . . is to listen and practise. Listen and practise, and your pronunciation will get better.'

'Listen and practise!' Ibrahim yelled happily.

But of course he wasn't really listening.

Sightseeing with Mr Ibrahim the next day turned out to be like some kind of bizarre fraternity initiation or religious penance. As we walked through the old Crusader castle and Roman ruins at Byblos, Mr Ibrahim demanded that I peek into every single tomb, climb every single rampart, and photograph every single colonnade. 'When will you come to Lebanon again?' Mr Ibrahim would shout every time I tried to complain about this. 'This is the history of my country!' As we walked from ruin to ruin, Mr Ibrahim wanted to know my opinion about each detail of the experience, and he got grumpy whenever he thought I wasn't being enthusiastic enough.

Amid this tireless touristic browbeating, I slowly learned things about my hellbent host. Mr Ibrahim, I discovered, was thirty-two years old, and the son of a Sunni Muslim father and a Maronite Christian mother. As a child, he and his family lived on the Green Line, and the young Ibrahim came to admire the American soldiers who patrolled his neighbourhood. Sometimes, the soldiers would give him vacuum-wrapped MREs (Meals, Ready-to-Eat) – dehydrated army food that tasted like chicken or beef or coffee. Ibrahim idolised the foreign soldiers, and – much to the consternation of his family – he hung a small American flag in his bedroom. Eventually, the Americans withdrew from Beirut, and Ibrahim's home was destroyed in the ongoing fighting. Salvaging what they could, he and his family moved in with relatives on the outskirts of town.

After the fighting subsided in 1990, Mr Ibrahim went into business, first selling simple household items within Lebanon and later importing goods from overseas. He first became rich by introducing certain European detergents and soaps to the Lebanese market, and that remained his main line of business – even though he spoke of branching out into jewellery and women's shoes.

If there was something in which Mr Ibrahim took the most pride, however, it was the fact that he had not so much as touched a girl in all of his thirty-two years. When we travelled back down the coast toward Jounieh, I quizzed him about this, and by the time we'd taken the cable car up to the Christian shrine at Harissa,

Mr Ibrahim was happily ranting about his utter lack of a sex life. As we climbed the winding staircase to the huge Virgin Mary statue, Mr Ibrahim told heroic stories of celibacy with the same lusty enthusiasm most men reserve for tales of sexual conquest.

'I've had thirty different women who wanted to do sex with me, and I told them all no!' Mr Ibrahim bellowed proudly, startling a group of Sri Lankan pilgrims as we spiralled our way up to the bronze Virgin. 'Some of them rented hotel rooms for me! One of them showed me her panties! But do you know what I told her?'

'What did you tell her?' I asked wearily.

'I told her no!'

Oddly enough, Mr Ibrahim was equally preoccupied with people who were highly promiscuous. Adbul the Bodyguard, he repeatedly reminded me, had fathered two children out of wedlock. During his days as a competitive body builder, Abdul had once had sex with five different women over the span of three days. Another associate of Mr Ibrahim's, a sixty-year-old Saudi man, had supposedly been married to eighty different women, and had fathered forty-two kids. This man's latest wife was a seventeen-year-old Syrian girl, and on their wedding night he'd taken Viagra and had sex with her eighteen times. After that night, Mr Ibrahim noted happily, the Saudi man had been paralysed for three days.

After Jounieh and Harissa, Mr Ibrahim had Adbul drive us back to Beirut. At first I thought this meant I would finally get to go home, but instead we ended up cruising the city for two hours. Meticulously avoiding war-damaged areas, Mr Ibrahim pointed out signs of the prosperous new Lebanon: shopping malls, cinemas, resort hotels and luxury high-rises. 'Look!' he would holler obsessively. 'This is just like Europe!'

Amid all his shouting, Mr Ibrahim seemed to be a man who very earnestly wanted to erase all the reputation and memories from a war that had ravaged his home. Somehow, through sheer force of personality, he hoped to turn Lebanon back into a booming, Westernised country. And I think he saw me as a kind of captive emissary who could bring the good news back to America.

Consequently, I shouldn't have been surprised when he arrived unannounced at my hotel the following morning, ranting about all the thousands of dollars in business he was passing up just so he could take me to the Chouf Mountains. Out of obligation, interpersonal cowardice, and lack of a ready excuse, I consented.

About five minutes out of Beirut, however, the presence of a Syrian military checkpoint got Mr Ibrahim off onto an anti-Syria diatribe that hadn't let up by the time we'd entered the mountains. The solution to the Syrian military and political presence in Lebanon, he'd reasoned, was to have the United States bomb the bejesus out of Damascus. After he'd demanded for the twenty-third time that I write a letter to President Clinton in support of this diplomatic strategy, I pointed out that – technically – he could go to the White House website and write that letter himself.

Less than one hour later, our plans to visit Beiteddine Palace had been summarily scrapped and I found myself taking dictation from Mr Ibrahim in a West Beirut Internet café.

'Do you have an email reply address?' I asked him. 'It's required if you're going to send a message to the White House.'

'Of course!' he boomed. 'I use email for business all the time.'

'Okay, then what is it?'

'What is what?'

'Your email address.'

Mr Ibrahim grinned and fluttered his eyelids. 'I have many email addresses – ten, maybe twenty email addresses.'

'Just give me one.'

Mr Ibrahim's grin wavered a bit. 'I don't remember.'

'Okay,' I said diplomatically, 'we'll use mine.'

By the time we were ready to type the body of the message, Mr Ibrahim was visibly nervous. 'What do I say?' he demanded testily.

'It's your message,' I replied. 'Tell him what's on your mind.'

'Dear President Clinton,' he dictated. 'It is my great pleasure and honour to write to you today, and if you ever come to Lebanon, I will be your tour guide and I will show you that we are a rich and beautiful country, and that we are not terrorists like you think we are.' Mr Ibrahim paused for a moment. 'Is that good?'

'Sure,' I said, keying in his greeting. 'It's your message, so say what you want.'

Mr Ibrahim grinned thoughtfully and stroked his goatee. 'Why do you support Israel when you ignore Lebanon?' he said. 'Are we not as good at business as them? Are we not more fashionable? Do we not love America also? So why do you give them a billion dollars while we are being invaded by Syrians, who hate America and smell like dogs?'

'Whoa, slow down,' I said, but Mr Ibrahim had already gone manic.

'When Saddam Hussein invaded Kuwait, you bombed Baghdad!' he yelled. 'So why not bomb Damascus now?'

I typed as fast as I could, wincing at Mr Ibrahim's reckless bravado. In a way, there was a certain sadness to what he was saying. Though created under circumstances similar to Israel, the nation of Lebanon has always been too small, disorganised and divided to avoid getting bullied by its neighbours.

'Look at us!' Mr Ibrahim hollered. 'Look at the people in this room! We are like Americans! We are like Europeans! We need business and tourists in Lebanon! We need the pope and Michael Jackson to come and see our faces . . .'

'I think that's enough for now,' I interjected.

'I am not finished!' he yelled indignantly.

'The president is a busy man,' I said sagely. 'It's best to keep it short.'

'Yes, you are right,' Mr Ibrahim said, looking a bit dazed. 'Do you think he will write back?'

The next day, Mr Ibrahim had to work, so I visited the village of Qana, near the zone in South Lebanon occupied until recently by Israel.

But, of course, it wasn't that simple. The night before, Mr Ibrahim had asked me what I was going to do in his absence, and when I told him Qana, he'd nearly lost it.

'You should not go to Qana!' he'd yelled. 'There is nothing to see there!'

By 'nothing to see', Mr Ibrahim meant that the place was a reminder of war. In Qana, the main tourist attraction is a Syrian-built memorial to the two hundred civilians who died when Israel shelled the town in 1996. However, since Qana is also one of the possible locations of Cana – where Jesus was said to have turned water into wine at a wedding festival – I was able to use this seemingly pious pretext to convince Mr Ibrahim of my good intentions.

Insisting that I also visit Sidon during my southbound trek, Mr Ibrahim gave me twenty dollars to cover transportation and admission fees. Each time I tried to refuse the twenty dollars, Mr Ibrahim accused me of not really wanting to go to Sidon. This accusation, of course, was completely valid. I finally convinced Mr Ibrahim to keep the money, but he made me promise to call him with a full report as soon as I got home that evening.

By the time I'd taken two buses and a share-taxi down to Qana, the comparative serenity of travelling without Mr Ibrahim had already made the trip worthwhile. Once in the town, I was more impressed by the sight of daily life in southern Lebanon than I was with the clumsy Syrian memorial to Israeli atrocity. South Lebanon is a predominately Shiite Muslim area, and huge pictures of the Ayatollah Khomeini hung on buildings and along roadsides. Some neighbourhoods flew the yellow flag of Hezbollah, while others displayed the green Amal flag. Despite the violent fanaticism associated with such symbols, however, the town itself went about its business at a casual, friendly pace.

Resolving to overcome my instinctive fear of all the Hezbollah iconography in the area, I hiked out into the countryside beyond the town. After about fifteen minutes of walking along a dusty road, I came to a UN roadblock manned by a couple of Fijian peacekeepers who introduced themselves as Vasco and Reef. The Fijians were stationed there as part of the UN Interim Force in Lebanon (UNIFIL), a mission which – despite its temporary-sounding name – has been in operation since the first Israeli invasion more than two decades ago.

After chatting with the blue-bereted soldiers for a couple of minutes, a loud explosion rang out, and a plume of smoke rose up from a hill on the horizon.

'Israelis?' I asked the Fijians nervously.

'No,' Vasco laughed. 'A rock quarry.'

'How can you tell the difference?'

'Well, the Israelis usually call on the radio before they start shelling us.'

Vasco encouraged me to hang out at the checkpoint for a while, and Reef went up to the watchtower to prepare some tea. Both Fijians seemed desperate to talk to someone who was fluent in English, and I was certainly thrilled to speak with someone who let me finish my sentences. When Reef returned with cups of milky tea and toast, the three of us chatted about politics, rugby and whether or not Jesus actually came to Qana. Reef was convinced that Jesus had turned the water into wine here in Lebanon; Vasco insisted that the miracle had happened at Kafr Kanna in Israel.

After a while, a couple of local teenagers walked up to greet the Fijians, and Vasco encouraged them to give me a tour of the area. Mahmoud, the older one, jogged off down the road and came back ten minutes later in his father's car.

'Mahmoud,' I said as I got into the car. 'Is that a Muslim name?'

'Yes, I am Sunni. But many of my friends are Christians. Maybe you've heard bad things about Lebanon, but we all get along in my town.'

'What about Shiites, do you get along with them?'

'Yes, the Shiites are good people. But they don't like sin, so sometimes they stay to themselves.'

'So does that mean you're a sinner?'

'Yes,' Mahmoud said seriously. 'I like to sin very much.'

After showing me some Roman-era Christian caves on the far side of Qana, Mahmoud took me to an archaeological dig that contained a couple of ancient stone wine vats. A third stone urn sat, broken, at the edge of the pit.

'Were these used to turn water into wine?' I asked Mahmoud.

'I don't know,' he said, 'but I know they are very old. I feel bad for breaking that one.' He pointed to the fractured urn at the edge of the pit.

'That urn is enormous,' I laughed. 'How could you have possibly broken it?'

'Well, my father owns a construction company, and I broke it with his bulldozer when we were building a street a couple of weeks ago. I thought it was a rock until we took it out of the ground.'

I looked again at the broken urn. Archaeologists go for years without finding anything that big or old, and here Mahmoud had discovered it doing his after-school job.

That evening, I returned to Beirut in good spirits. Buoyed by my successful foray into the south of Lebanon, I went out for an evening stroll through East Beirut and ended up stumbling upon (though not entirely by accident) none other than the Hole in the Wall pub. There, I drank a couple of beers and listened to music until just short of ten o'clock.

When I arrived back at my hotel, Mr Ibrahim and Abdul the Bodyguard were in the lobby waiting for me. I noticed that Mr Ibrahim was cradling an enormous plastic tub full of pudding.

'I told you to call me!' he bellowed as soon as he caught sight of me.

'Yes, well I was just going to call . . .'

'Where have you been?'

'Well, I started out by going to Qana . . .'

'Qana? What about Sidon?'

At this point, I was too flustered to do anything but lie outright. 'Sidon,' I said. 'Well, wow! It was great.'

'What did you see there?'

'The ruins. I visited the ruins.' This was a stab in the dark; for all I knew, the big attraction in Sidon was a Tijuana-style donkey show.

'The ruins!' Mr Ibrahim yelled. I wasn't sure what this meant until he grinned and held up the tub of pudding. 'My sister made you some sweets!' he said. 'We can eat it together.'

Relieved at being off the hook, I plopped down next to Mr Ibrahim and started to spoon up the chocolate dessert. After a couple of bites, Mr Ibrahim tugged the bowl away from me.

'You smell like Al Cole,' he said. One couch over, Adbul diplomatically picked up a magazine and pretended to read it.

'Al Cole?'

'Did you drink al-coal tonight?'

It dawned on me what he meant. 'Just a couple of beers,' I said.

'In Sidon?' Mr Ibrahim yelled.

'Um, no,' I mumbled. 'I had them here in Beirut.'

'You didn't call me because . . . you . . . were . . . drinking . . . al-coal?' Mr Ibrahim glowered at me. Obviously, this was a major betrayal in his moral world.

'Like I said, I was going to . . .'

'I have been waiting here for two hours!'

'Well, you didn't need to come all the way . . .'

Mr Ibrahim shoved the tub of pudding over at me. 'You eat this,' he said quietly. 'I'm not hungry any more.'

'I'm sorry, it's just –'

'Eat it!'

'Doesn't Abdul want –'

'Abdul is not hungry either!'

I stared down at the pudding. The plastic tub was so big that I could have used it to smuggle a bowling ball through customs at the airport. There was no way I could have eaten all of it by myself, and I secretly suspected that he'd had his sister prepare it with the sole intention of punishing me for not calling him within the proper time frame.

Gripping my spoon, I made my best effort. As I choked down the chocolate dessert, it occurred to me that my weird friendship with Mr Ibrahim betrayed my own credulous, middle-class sense of judgement. Had someone as ruthless and narrow as Mr

Ibrahim been a penniless street sweeper with a donkey cart and a chicken instead of a Mercedes and a bodyguard, I doubt I'd have accepted his efforts to help me in the first place – and I certainly wouldn't have let him know where I was staying. But seeing Lebanon by Mercedes and eating gourmet meals had made me rationalise Mr Ibrahim's idiosyncrasies. Somehow, I suspect that both his social life and his moral self-concept depended on people like me.

In the end, Mr Ibrahim never did force me to eat all of the pudding. After verifying to his satisfaction that I was truly suffering from the effort, he melodramatically forgave me for not calling him, then went home for the night.

If he had any intention of surprising me with a sightseeing trek the next day, I didn't wait around to find out. Immediately after the pudding incident, I wrote Mr Ibrahim a note. It read: 'I'm sorry to have to tell you this way, but I had to go to Syria on short notice. Thank you for your kindness and hospitality. I will remember Lebanon well.'

The following morning, I left the note with the manager of my hotel and took the first bus up the coast to Tripoli. For the first hour of the bus ride, I had trouble relaxing: I kept expecting the old lady in the seat next to me to pull off a polyurethane face mask and reveal herself, grinning madly, as Mr Ibrahim.

As for the note I left with the hotel manager, it wasn't completely dishonest: I will indeed remember Lebanon well.

It's just that too much of any good thing has a way of wearing a man down.

We Can't Fix Anything, Even the Smallest Things, in Cuba

DAVE EGGERS

Dave Eggers is the editor of *McSweeney's*, a quarterly and a book-publishing company, and is the author of two books: *A Heartbreaking Work of Staggering Genius* and *You Shall Know Our Velocity*. In 2002 he founded 826 Valencia, a San Francisco educational non-profit organisation for kids, focussing on literacy.

I HAVE A STORY that fits the theme of this book. Actually, I have a dozen of them, but most of them involve help with flat tyres or directions, so I'll go with a more nuanced story that fits the theme, though not neatly.

I was in Cuba with my friend Marny, writing for a magazine about the impressions one might get of the Cuban people in a short time, on the cusp of the millennium. To do this, Marny and I drove around the island for ten days in late 1999, over hills and under clouds, in the cities and the country, picking up hitchhikers, talking to them, asking questions without prying too much, and then dropping them off at their destinations. We met about seventy people, each and every one – those who we spoke to, at least – unfailingly kind. At one point the starting centre for the Cuban national basketball team hitched a ride from outer Havana to her apartment – absolutely true; I have pictures – and we were invited in, and were soon offered a place to stay. There's no more hospitable country on the planet, I would guess.

On the first day, though, before we'd even rented a car, we were walking along the Malecón, and the ocean was bursting over the wall, over the road, spray everywhere, frozen above us, momentarily, in the sun. The wind was gusting, and we sat for a second under a statue (of whom I wish I now knew), watching a group of boys play stickball. [Side note: I'm writing this far after the actual deadline and months after I turned in my first contribution, which involved a taxi driver in Copenhagen – and which really wasn't all that great a story. Long after writing that and turning it in, this other tale hit me, and I'm getting it down in one night, right under the deadline, so you have to forgive any overt evidence of its rushed execution. Had I more time – and if it really mattered to the story – I'd chase down the name of the statue. But for now let's say it was of Carol Channing.]

The wind suddenly brought a bunch of pages our way, and we got up and reflexively started running around, chasing the pages down. After we gathered ten or so of the papers, we noticed a small boy helping us, and his parents coming just after him. The papers were his, it became clear; they were his homework, it seemed. A few pages disappeared across the plaza and onto and over the Malecón, past the fishermen and into the sea, but we got most of them, and together we all sat down, where Marny and I had been sitting in the first place, under Carol Channing.

The couple was young, married, and their son was about seven. They introduced themselves, but the only name I can guarantee at this point was that of the father: Vladimir. The couple was bright, charming, and their son, whom I'll call Ruben, was the very face of hopeful youth. We told them we were tourists, had just arrived that day via Cancún (on a plane full of already-drunk Club Med vacationers), and were spending our first day wandering, with no particular plans, not even a map.

And then, after we had been chatting no more than two to four minutes, Vladimir and his wife, who shall be known as Maria, invited us to eat lunch at their house. Worldly travellers will know that a) this happens from time to time in some countries, but that b) it doesn't happen in the US, and it rarely happens anywhere in Europe, or really any industrialised country, for that matter. Marny and I were both from a small Chicago suburb, and people there were friendly enough, but to this day I've never been anywhere in the US where someone would invite just-met tourists to their home for lunch. But this is what was happening, and it was all the more startling given that these people, from what we could quickly guess/ascertain from Ruben's well-worn shoes and ratty backpack, were not a pair of eccentric millionaires. We haggled for a few minutes about the plan, and decided eventually that instead of lunch we would do dinner.

Marny and I debated in English, out of earshot, about the economics of the dinner. We didn't feel right allowing them to buy us a meal, but weren't sure if they'd accept our contribution to the necessary groceries. We took a chance and Marny made the offer. Vladimir, to our surprise, immediately accepted, and without hesitation told us that about twenty American dollars would do the trick. We gave him the money and he gave us the phone number of his apartment building – they didn't have their own phone – and drew us a map to their place.

That afternoon, as Marny and I walked around, we broke down the encounter, asking questions and guessing at their answers.

Question One: Why would this family invite strangers into their home?

Answer One: We seem harmless, probably, and perhaps they don't have many friends. Maybe they love Americans. Maybe they're just curious people, thrill-seekers. Maybe they're swingers.

Questions Two and Three: Why would they need twenty dollars for the food, when the exchange rate at the time meant that twenty dollars would last them about a month? Wouldn't they know that we knew this, and that our knowing this would possibly sour our goodwill towards them?

Answers Two and Three: They probably don't care. Chances are, they know that we know that twenty dollars is a huge amount of money under the circumstances, and they know that we know that they'll be able to buy everything they need for the night for about two dollars. But they know that we know that this twenty dollars means comparatively little to us, that in the US a chicken and a bottle of wine would cost around that amount, and that we wouldn't mind paying even twice this much in exchange for their hospitality and an evening of lively conversation.

Which is what we got. When we showed up, we gave Ruben a model aeroplane we'd bought on the way, and presented them with a bottle of wine we'd picked up, too, for the equivalent of $2.60. Vladimir and Maria and Ruben lived in a one-and-a-half-room apartment in a complex of about eighty units, all set around a small rectangular courtyard that received no direct light. The doors separating them from the outdoor hallway were like shutters, such that much of what happened elsewhere in the complex could be heard inside.

In the family area of their apartment, there was a couch, a chair, a small television set and a small portable stereo, both on a rolling TV stand. A few feet into the apartment was the kitchen, and before it, a table and four folding chairs. The table was set, and Maria was busy with the dinner preparations. Ruben was playing with his new plane, and Marny and I, sitting on the couch, complimented the family on their place. Their home was clean and pleasant.

But the thing that all travellers at first find shocking when invited into such homes – and I've experienced this in villages along the Amazon, in hovels in Cairo, in huts in Senegal, on and on – is the lack of *things*. This couple was about thirty years old, and their son seven, and yet they had accumulated almost no *things*. There were no books, no magazines, no newspapers, few toys, no trinkets, no baubles, no tapes or records or CDs, only one small picture on the wall, of I can't remember what; we could have counted the objects in the room on two hands. Even in a country like Cuba, certainly not a nation of materialists, it seemed inexplicable that over so many years there would be so little evidence of having and keeping, even of objects of purely personal value. But then again, maybe they were just neat people, and their stuff was in the closet.

Before we ate dinner and after we ate dinner, while Maria was relatively quiet, Vladimir talked, primarily in English. And Vladimir had things on his mind. Right away he brought out the tool of his trade: he made cigars at one of the state-owned factories and what he showed us was a wooden mould, made of two halves, with room for about six cigars. The mould looked hundreds of years old, and might very well have been. He described how he made the cigars, how much they brought on the world market – a great deal – and how much each of the factory's employees made in return – almost nothing. This, he said, made no sense and had nothing to do with the way things were supposed to be in Cuba.

We asked about the origin of his name, whether Russian names were common. He said common enough, that his father was Vladimir, too, so named because his grandfather had fought for the revolution, side by side with Che Guevara, with Russian guns.

But this, he said, sweeping his arm across the room, was not what his grandfather had fought for. It was time, he said, for Fidel to step down. He had lost his grip. The people were not behind him any more. It was time for capitalism, he said, time for tourism and foreign investment. People like Vladimir and his family could not live like this for much longer.

He pointed to his TV. How did he get that? he asked. We didn't know. From another tourist, he said. There was no way he could afford it on his pay. Another tourist, an older man whom he'd met a year ago, had bought it for them while he was in town. Everything that anyone has, Vladimir said, comes from elsewhere. This tourist friend of theirs had later sent them money, and an uncle of his in Miami had sent them money, but otherwise there was not enough to get by on. All the money anyone in Cuba had, he said, came from family living in the US or Europe. How long did they have to live this way? This was not, he repeated then and often during the course of the night, what his grandfather had fought for! He fought next to Che for this?

Vladimir was standing up as he spoke. He was loud and clearly agitated but also loving the sound of his own voice and opinions, and we wondered how he could be so fearless with his views in a building like his, where the next apartment was separated from his by no more than drywall and a shutter-like door, where there were perhaps three hundred residents within earshot, none of them more than twenty-five metres from his door.

We ate, and the food – chicken and rice – was fine. Marny and I shared a smile when we realised that Vladimir and Maria hadn't even bought one whole chicken; the four of us were sharing one half-chicken, accompanied by a scoop of rice each, while Ruben was still playing. He'd apparently eaten earlier.

After dinner the whole family walked us to our next destination, a cabaret club we'd read about in our guidebook. The air was humid and good, but it had been a long night – Vladimir had talked for an hour or so after dinner, too – and we were ready for some mindless entertainment. But it was clear that Vladimir wasn't ready to allow us to part company forever. He asked for, and we gave him, the name of the hotel where we were staying (after he'd offered to put us up in his apartment; he and his family could stay at a relative's, he said). He asked about our plans for the next day (we were driving to Cienfuegos), and the next (we didn't know yet). He wanted us to come to dinner again, or lunch, or anything. His family could show us the beaches, or Hemingway's bay, or whatever we wanted. He wanted our address in the US, and a phone number, and gave us his again, while standing on the cobblestone street outside the club, everyone bathed in neon.

His eyes were trying to be kind, friendly and even casual, but there was a desperation there, and I had the feeling that if we didn't buy them something like a TV, sooner or later we would be in arrears. But we didn't have enough cash with us to hand them anything, and so we told them we'd come back sometime in the next week – we still had the map and their number – before we left. The implication was that we'd have another meal together, and with us we'd bring gifts, perhaps a new stereo, for he'd made the point clearly that their current one was broken. And that they had no working fan. And that they hadn't eaten beef in a year.

Sitting inside the club, Marny and I already felt hung over. We were trapped inside the wretched and unavoidable dilemma every traveller knows: there were people here we could help immeasurably, who had implied their need for our help in particular; they had chosen us. But we had not chosen them. Why had we not chosen them? I have no idea.

Over the course of the week, we gave a good deal of money to a lot of people we met, but we never visited Vladimir and Maria again. And I wish at this point I could clearly articulate why. My first guess is that we felt that our responsibility was too muddled, that their interest in us was clearly mercenary, that in many ways we were being played. Who knows how often the pair of them used hospitality for gain? We might have been the hundredth and hundredth-and-first travellers they'd ensnared with their beautiful son;

it seemed possible that they in fact trolled for people like us, always in the shadow of Carol Channing, always with the same m.o.

We eased ourselves with these assumptions, but three years on, I have a different thesis, why we didn't call them again, didn't visit them again. My thesis: that our responsibility towards them was actually not muddled at all, but all too clear. As humans with means – our connecting flight from Cancún to Havana cost more than Vladimir would make in half a year – we were morally obliged to share it with his family. Not because they had fed us, or welcomed us into their home, but because we had simply met them. At two in the morning, as I write these words, I don't even think this is such a radical idea: that meeting people and knowing of their suffering obligates those able to help to do just that. And I think Marny and I knew this. We had become involved with this family, and our duty was clear: we should have done what we could have, given the time and means available, to make their lives more comfortable. And the only excuse I can now offer for why we didn't was that there was no intrinsic circumscription to our involvement.

What would be enough? When would we have satisfied our moral responsibility? A purist, like myself at 2 a.m., would say not until they were living at a level similar to our own. It would involve more visits, care packages, wire transfers, and even, to take it to the logical end, any help we could offer to help them leave the island. And why, again, were we thus responsible? Because we knew them, and knew how their lives might be improved. Knowledge of their situation is tantamount to obligation.

But we didn't call them again, as I've said. At one point during the trip, we gave a ride to a young woman who we learned was a huge fan of Michael Bolton. We promised to send her all the Michael Bolton swag we could get our hands on in the US, and eventually we did. That was something within our power, our comprehension, something we could fit within our schedules.

I ended up exploring these themes in a novel I wrote a few years later, but I still don't have helpful answers or a plan that would work in all situations – or any situation, really. To stay pure, to equalise the economic disparity between you and everyone you might meet – and you know there is a simple beauty to that aim, not to mention a visceral appeal – you would need, among many other things, a lot of time. So there's no room for a categorical imperative here. There's no room for doing what you need to do. There's room only to do what you want to do, with your head a hive of guilt.

Losing It in London

DOUGLAS CRUICKSHANK

Douglas Cruickshank's work has appeared in *Travel & Leisure*, Salon.com, the *Readerville Journal*, various newspapers and *Salon.com's Wanderlust: Real-life Tales of Adventure and Romance*. He lives near San Francisco.

THE THING I LIKE about London cab drivers, besides their endless idiosyncratic erudition, is that nine out of ten of them are an unmitigated hoot. They are at least as funny as most of the stand-up comedians you see on late-night TV. They're splendid improvisers and they do it while navigating the madness of London streets.

Take my current cabbie, for instance, with whom I'm stuck in rush-hour traffic in the usual glorpy British weather. In the first five minutes I'm in his cab, George ('Name's George, call me George for short') informs me that his hobbies are entomology – he belongs to a club that hatches and releases butterflies and moths – and mystery writing. I'm not a mystery writer, but I've read my share, and when I was a kid I had a large collection of butterflies, moths and tropical beetles, so George and I hit it off.

'I write short stories at night, mysteries usually,' he tells me, 'because there's never anything I want to watch on the tube.' We talk about my unwieldy Scottish surname for a few minutes, but once he finds out I'm from the US, he starts going on about Elmore Leonard. And when I say I'm writing a story about London and comment on the rain, he tells me that Elmore Leonard says you should never start a story by describing the weather.

'"Never open a book with weather," is what he actually said,' George tells me. 'But I guess that would go for, you know, any length story you were writing – wouldn't have to be a book.'

'Okay,' I say. 'How about this: "I'm in the back of a taxi in London and I did not recently fall into the Thames or any other body of water, but I look as if I did."'

'That'll do,' George says. 'I think that might get past old Elmore.'

'But why can't you start a story with weather?'

'You simply cannot,' he says. 'Elmore Leonard says so. It's one of his rules.'

'Well, if Elmore Leonard told you you had to start a story by blowing someone's brains out, would you do it?'

'I would indeed, sir. By all means.'

Come to think of it, that is a pretty good beginning for a story.

I guess Mr Leonard has a point. Most people are more likely to keep reading a story that opens with brains being blown out than a story that starts with, say, a breezy drizzle near Piccadilly Circus, or a leaf fluttering past during a gale, or a guy riding in a cab through a rainstorm.

After forty gruelling minutes of crawling through London at a pace that makes it seem like all the cars have filled up on Demerol instead of gasoline, George is on a roll, and I'm trying to keep up with him.

'Would you stop at that bank up there on the left? I need to go to the ATM,' I say. 'So I can go buy you a gun.'

'Har!' George says and slaps the wheel. 'You don't want to put a gun in my hand, mate. Not in this traffic.' He pulls up at the bank nonetheless and I get out and ask him to wait. 'Don't forget the silencer,' he yells to me. See what I mean? What a card.

First thing tomorrow morning, I'm scheduled to leave for Leicester, about an hour north, where I'm to stay on a spectacular old country estate. I'll get besotted on expensive single malt Scotch, refuse to smoke expensive cigars, and run into Mariah Carey who's in a room down the hall. But that's an entirely different story that doesn't really have anything to do with this one, except that the Leicester expedition is the reason I'm stopping at the ATM. I'm withdrawing 160 pounds so that I won't have to deal with hunting down an ATM once we're in the hunt country. A reasonable enough thing to do, no? That's what I thought.

I've spent the day sightseeing all over London, picking up gifts, visiting the London Silver Vaults, the Victoria & Albert Museum, the Buckingham Palace shop, John Soane's eccentric museum on Lincoln's Inn Fields and countless small stores trading in everything from tea and tea paraphernalia to large animal skulls mounted on polished marble bases. I've also stopped into one or more pubs to partake of invigorating beverages. In addition to a black canvas shoulder bag in which I carry a notebook, camera and maps, I'm lugging around several large bags of booty for friends and family back home. And I've bought myself a book –

The Power of the Poster, a catalogue for the show on the history of posters I saw at the V & A, which I've been using as a writing desk as George and I compose our story. Now, as I stand at the ATM while it spits out money, I realise I've still got the book in my hand. Thanks to the little round mirror to my left, I'm also aware that there's a line of four people behind me and several others – not entirely reputable looking – milling around in the vicinity and showing an unwholesome interest in my ATM transaction. Consequently, I quickly tuck my fistful of cash under the front cover of *The Power of the Poster* instead of pulling out my over-stuffed wallet and trying to cram the wee fortune in amongst all the dollars, pound notes, old dry cleaning receipts and bent business cards.

We're far enough into this account that I suppose even Mr Leonard would permit me a direct reference to the weather: it's fucking pouring. I trot to the car from the ATM, but get drenched anyway. Once we get out in the sludge-like flow of traffic, George says, 'Now, read me that first line and I'll come up with another.'

'Something to advance the plot,' I say.

'Well, of course, mate,' he replies.

I read it to him: 'I'm in the back of a taxi in London and I did not recently fall into the Thames or any other body of water, but I look as if I did.'

'Here's your second sentence,' he says. '"I glance down to my lap and notice that my left hand is free of wounds, but covered in blood."'

Sheesh, this guy does sit down and write mysteries every night. I'm not going to be able to keep up. I jot down his contribution to the story and my brain grinds to a halt.

He looks at me in the rear-view mirror. 'You still back there?'

'I'm thinking, I'm thinking,' I say. There's a long silence. I see him watching me in the mirror. I also see the Royal Garden Hotel, where I've been staying the last couple of days, about a block away. The rain has stopped, so have all the cars. I've got it.

'Third and fourth sentences: "I look up to see the driver watching me in the rear-view mirror. He's wearing sunglasses even though it's 11 p.m."'

George gives me the thumbs-up sign. The traffic is at a complete standstill. 'I hate to end this brilliant collaboration,' I say, 'but I think I'll just hop out here.' I put down the book I've been using as a desk, tuck my notebook in my canvas bag, pull out my wallet, hand him the fare and a fat tip, grab my bags and dash for the curb just as the traffic starts moving.

He winks when I hand him the fare. 'We'll finish that story on the next ride, mate.' A charming fellow.

As I approach my hotel I see a dozen or more police officers around the front door and another five or six motorcycle cops sitting in the driveway that loops up to the entrance from Kensington High Street. Japanese Prime Minister Ryutaro Hashimoto, French President Jacques Chirac and rap star Busta Rhymes are all staying at the Royal Garden. It's a combo that's given the management a big-time case of the nerves. They're all high-maintenance guests, but Rhymes and entourage seem to rattle the hotel officials even more than the world leaders do. The cops are here to escort Hashimoto and Chirac in and out of their Rover Sterling sedans, and to and from their conference, which is being held a couple of miles away. The Rhymes bunch sometimes hangs out in the lobby, flopped over chairs and couches, engaged in perfectly harmless banter at a volume that drives the front desk attendants up the wall, but also injects a little life into the church-like reception area. Yesterday, Chirac and his bodyguards walked through and he eyed the noisy, elaborately outfitted Rhymes contingent with fascination, amusement and envy. They're obviously having much more fun than he is. By all accounts he's a guy who likes a good time and being cooped up with a bunch of presidents and prime ministers all day must be about as dull as life can get.

When I enter the lobby, several security types – tight-suited sleeve-talkers with tiny earphones and curly cords that snake down inside their collars – look at my half-dozen bags with alarm but do nothing. I nod to the desk attendant, who nods back, and I walk to the elevator.

I'm pooped. I get to my room, throw the bags on the bed and kick off my shoes with the thought that I'll relax and dry out for a while before dinner. I'll page through the book I bought at the V & A.

Oh, shit! Where is the book?

I look through the bags. I look under the bags. I look in the chair and next to the bed and on the nightstand and under the wet pants I've thrown on the coffee table. But I know it's no use. I see the little movie playing in my brain – the one where I bound out of the cab with everything except the book; the book with my ATM loot in it, all 160 pounds worth. Damn.

Okay. Remain calm. No problem. There are only about 19,000 cabs in London. I didn't catch the number of mine, nor the driver's last name. Excellent. Terrific. I'm in good shape. I need a drink immediately. Or a walk. Or both. I put my shoes and damp pants back on and leave the room. I exit the hotel, make my way through the flock of constables, and walk across Kensington High Street muttering curses to myself and racking my brain for a solution. I don't find one, but I do find a pub, which is the next best thing.

It's called The Goat, but with better luck it might be called The Elusive Camel, The Queens Head and Artichoke, The Moon Under Water or any of a jillion other lyrical names given to drinking establishments in this country. Some of them seem so much like a line snatched from haiku that I wonder if pub naming has been appropriated by the government as an employment program for versifiers. Or maybe it's just that the pub naming standard has been raised so high that the onerous responsibility of naming a new one brings out the poet in pub owners. What other explanation could there be for monikers like The Eagle and Child, The Balloon Up the Creek, The Startled Saint and The Pig In Paradise?

I order a Guinness and stand at the bar. There are only about a dozen people in the place. I suck the foam off the top of my glass, stare into space and feel sorry for myself. What a fucking fool I am. And I'm stumped. There's no way of finding that cab that I can think of. I finish the Guinness in three gulps and order another. Eavesdropping is my favourite pastime when alone at bars or restaurants and I'm doing it now. The two blokes next to me are having a heated conversation but it's tough to listen in because they seem to be talking gobbledygook.

The taller one says emphatically, '*Acherontia atropos.*'

His shorter friend tries to repeat it, '*Acherontia apropos.*'

'No, not *apropos*, *atropos*. *Acherontia atropos.*'

'Got it,' the short bloke says, but he doesn't try to say it again.

'Or, ya know, mate, just "Death's Head" is fine, too. That's the common name,' the tall one says as he glances at me and notices I'm staring at them. 'You interested in moths?' he asks me.

'Sorry,' I say. 'I just couldn't help trying to figure out what you were talking about.'

'Oh, yeah, we're moth nuts,' he says. 'Death's Head is a moth; big, handsome yellow and black fella. I was just telling him the Latin name. You're a Yank?'

'Yes, I am.'

'Enjoying London?'

'Mostly,' I say.

The two introduce themselves; the tall one's Ian, the shorter one's James. I tell them about my trip so far, the upcoming getaway to Leicester (James grew up there, so he reels off a list of 78-and-a-half things I must do or see, three of which I will end up doing or seeing) and I buy them each a drink; seems they've just gotten off work. Finally, after we've talked nonstop for maybe thirty minutes without ever descending into the so-what-do-you-do? bog, Ian says 'Mostly?'

'Huh?' I say.

'You said "mostly". You said you were enjoying London mostly.'

'Oh, well, it's no fault of London's but I just left 160 pounds in the cab I was riding in.'

'Ouch,' James says. 'How'd you manage that, mate?' I go through the whole story in excruciating detail, thanks to the Guinness. But Ian and James are also well lubricated so they listen raptly then start to laugh. They giggle a little at first, but then break out into full-blown chortles and I'm starting to get pissed off when Ian says, 'Well, mate, I can't think of a better cab to leave it in. That's got to be George, right James?' James nods enthusiastically. 'We're all in the same entomology club. He hatched, I think, four Death's Heads just last year. I mean, as many cabs as there are, there can't be two drivers who collect butterflies and moths, write mystery stories and are named George, can there now? He's been published a couple times, you know. I know him; James knows him, too. Not real well, but I think I know where I can get his number. I'll call him straight away. He's probably knocked off by now.'

I'm starting to think maybe there is a god. I mean, consider the odds: London's population of about seven million multiplied by 19,000 cabs divided by several dozen Kensington pubs I could have wandered into equals no way in hell I should have met not one, but two guys who know the guy who's got my 160 pounds and my book.

While James and I drink up and Ian goes off to call George, I think about other extraordinary strokes of luck that have floated through my life. Once, at Poipu Beach on Kauai, I was body-surfing and my girlfriend was lying on the sand. It was just before sunset. I came out of the water to find her slowly crawling around on the large grass mats we'd brought, peering at the ground.

'What are you doing?' I asked.

'I lost my contact.'

'You are shitting me!'

'I'm not, and I think it went in the sand.'

'I thought you were going to leave them in the room.'

'Just help me look for it. It's got a little blue dot, we might be able to see it.'

'It's got a little blue dot!'

'Don't start with me,' she said. I got on my knees and began looking.

In no time at all the Hawaiian sun had sunk behind the post-card horizon and darkness seemed to be galloping across the sky. We both had our noses to the beach, slowly, gingerly trying to find the lens, which was invisible, except, of course, for The Little Blue Dot. It was getting darker. It was virtually certain that if the thing was on top of the sand anywhere in the vicinity of our mats we would have inadvertently buried or crunched it by now. We were just about to give up while we could still find our way back to the car when her palm appeared in front of my face. 'Here it is!' she said. We each had three mai tais that night, which didn't make it different than any other night, but did make finding the lens seem even more miraculous than it was.

Then there's the story about a friend's family, back in the 1960s. They were travelling, with their dog, to Africa where the husband was going to take a job. They stopped off for a few days in Rome and on an evening walk, lost the dog. They looked and looked but couldn't find it. The next day, they had to leave for Africa, so off they went. Two years later they returned and again stopped for a few days in Rome. (You see where this is going, I'm sure.) One evening they walked through the same square where they lost the dog two years earlier. The husband, who had had a few drinks, called the dog's name. Out of the darkness, a scraggly, dirty but otherwise intact canine came trotting up to them and – you guessed it – it was their dog.

Everybody's got a couple of these stories, I suppose. Remarkable things do happen, which is why I'm not surprised to now hear Louis Armstrong coming out of a nearby speaker: 'And I think to myself what a wonderful world. Yes I think to myself what a wonderful world . . .' Now there's a song, I think to myself, that's never going to make it into an Elmore Leonard book. I signal to the bartender to order another round, and maybe I'll order another after that.

But wait, I had you going there, didn't I? I even had myself going. I was getting a little misty just at the thought of that doggie and family reunion. But you know and I know, and Mr

Leonard certainly knows, that it is not a wonderful world. It is a shit world and there is no god, especially today in glorpy, rainy London in The Goat pub, where I'm counting chickens in advance of their hatching, and buying the rounds even though I've lost 160 goddamn pounds.

Ian's walking back from the phone through the smoky room, and the big, toothy, red-nosed, alcohol-fuelled grin he's been wearing for the last forty minutes is nowhere in sight. He's slowly, mournfully shaking his head, though he does brighten a bit when the new round of drinks slides into place. 'Well,' he says. 'I've got some bad news and some bad news.'

James laughs. I do not. 'Okay,' I say. 'Let me have it.'

'George and his wife have gone to Blackpool to tend his mother; she's quite elderly, I understand, and they won't be back until day after tomorrow. It was just a message on their machine; they didn't leave a number.'

'Thanks for trying. I appreciate it.'

'I left a message explaining your predicament, but I don't know if they'll get it tonight. You might want this.' Ian jots down George's number on a paper coaster and hands it to me. Oh well, 160 pounds won't break me, but I wasn't planning to throw it away either.

James, Ian and I have another round of drinks. I tell them a long and tangled story about raising several Luna moths ('*Actias luna*,' Ian says) in my bedroom when I was a kid, and trying to train them. The pale green Lunas are docile, even friendly creatures, but furry as they are, they're not dogs. I finally gave up and let them go. 'I envy you, mate,' Ian says. 'I've never seen a live Luna.'

Naturally, we talk about politics and our jobs. James gets going on the seriously maudlin tale of his divorce – the kind of story you can virtually count on after several drinks with strangers – and Ian checks his watch and says his wife's going to divorce him if he doesn't get home. I leave with Ian, thank him again for his help, and walk back across the street to the hotel, resigned to my loss and, thanks to several hours worth of Guinness, not really very upset about it any longer.

In the Royal Garden's lobby the Rhymes gang is massing for some kind of evening outing. I'm in a downright chipper mood by this time and I give them a big smile, and two of the men return cool, friendly nods; the women stare at me blankly. A horrendous noise outside signals the arrival of the motorcycle escort for Chirac. There's about six of them, all wearing fluorescent yellow vests and looking officious. I decide to get to my room so I don't have to witness the desk clerk having a coronary, but as I zip past he says, 'Oh, Sir, I believe this came for you. This is you, correct?' he asks, pointing to my name written on a brown paper bag. 'A young woman brought it in a while ago, didn't leave her name.'

'That's me. Thank you.'

I open the bag and pull out *The Power of the Poster*. One hundred and sixty pounds slips out from under the front cover and falls to the floor along with a folded slip of paper.

I head to my room and sit on the bed, reading George's note: 'You left this. I think you might want it. Have a good trip, and remember, don't open with weather.'

I call the number Ian wrote on the coaster to leave a thank you message, but a young woman answers. It's Liz, George's daughter, the one who dropped off the book at the hotel. I thank her profusely and we chat for a few minutes. It turns out that she's just eighteen and that she had to drive nearly forty minutes to get to the hotel from the outlying suburb where they live. 'I got the message after my parents left,' Liz says. 'My dad had left the book on the kitchen table with a note saying if I was going into town, to drop it at the Royal Garden.' I thank her again. 'No worries,' she says. 'I didn't have anything else to do, and my boyfriend came with me and we, uh, stopped at a pub.'

For some reason, I ask her which pub she stopped at. It's a ridiculous question for an out-of-towner to ask a native because there are thousands of pubs in London and the place she went to would probably mean nothing to me. 'The Goat Tavern,' she says, naming the one pub that I actually know. We talk a little longer and figure out that she and her boyfriend were in the place while James, Ian and I were. Two or three couples came in that I noticed. They were one of them. 'That beats all,' Liz says. I thank her for the third or fourth time and we hang up.

I guess it is an okay world after all. Random as all hell, but sometimes, when you least expect it and least deserve it, randomly good. Amongst a billion billion grains of sand, a contact lens magically reappears; against all odds a long-lost dog shows up; in a city of seven million you just happen to run into the right strangers at the right time, and they happen to be fun to drink with and also have an interest in butterflies and moths; and a teenage girl goes out of her way to return a pile of money to an absent-minded dolt from another country whom she's never met, and gets to have a short interlude with her boyfriend at a pub called The Goat.

Andean High

GINGER ADAMS OTIS

Ginger Adams Otis is a freelance writer and frequent traveller living in the New York area. She is a contributing editor for the *Ex-Berliner* and writes for the *Village Voice, Ms., Jane, In These Times* and several other publications. She recently collected material for a number of upcoming essays while researching parts of Brazil for Lonely Planet's *South America on a Shoestring*.

ON A STICKY HOT June day about two years ago, I was sitting in a windowless office on the twenty-second floor of a Manhattan skyscraper parsing sentences when the phone rang. It was my good friend Lauren, calling to tell me that she, her brother Rich and his partner Rick were planning yet another fabulous trip to a far-flung location. I gritted my teeth as she chatted on about South America, and did rapid calculations as to what such a jaunt might cost (inevitably, more than I had). Then she mentioned Macchu Picchu, the long-abandoned stronghold of the Incan Empire hidden in the peaks of the Andes – a place I'd wanted to see since I was fifteen. 'Are you going to miss this one too?' a voice whispered inside my head. The answer came back immediately: absolutely not.

Less than a month later, on a sleepy Thursday afternoon, the four of us rolled into the desert oasis of San Pedro de Atacama in northern Chile. We'd been travelling for about two weeks, and time was growing short for me. I had to be back in New York by 1 August, so at some point I was going to have to head off on my own for Cuzco, the town nearest to Macchu Picchu, and from there to Lima for my flight home. The only problem was money – or rather, my almost total lack of it. Lauren, Rick and Rich were generously underwriting portions of my trip, but once I left them, it would be slim pickings.

But I wasn't thinking about that yet – I was still in the present, looking forward to a weekend of hiking the *altiplano*. We booked a package with a Dutch guide, who gave us a final word of stern advice: 'Altitude sickness is no joke. Drink lots of water, bring snacks for energy and, above all, do not drink alcohol.'

Why we didn't pay more attention to those words I'll never know – perhaps because we hadn't grasped that San Pedro itself is significantly above sea level. Not lung-squeezingly so, but high enough to have a creeping, debilitating effect on our bodies. During dinner Rick suggested a quick round of pisco sours to kick off our teetotaller's weekend. The fizzy drinks went down well in the dry desert air, and we unwisely ordered more. Soon the mud walls of the adobe hut fairly shook with our increasingly uninhibited laughter. It wasn't until Rich, normally a reserved fellow, nearly pitched into the open fire en route to the bathroom, and then made the return trip on his hands and knees that the penny dropped: we were rip-roaringly drunk on just two drinks.

The rest of the weekend was a study in Sisyphean torture: as we went higher, the headaches and dehydration worsened. Gulping water meant finding boulders to act as makeshift bathrooms. Just walking fifteen metres had us gasping and light-headed. When we tottered down from the last outing on Sunday afternoon and collapsed in the bus station, not one of us had a lick of energy left.

It was at this inauspicious moment that I decided to make my move. I hadn't booked the Cuzco portion of my trip yet and belatedly realised I'd left myself only four days to get there and then to Lima. While we waited for the bus to Calama, a medium-sized town about two hours away, I called the airline to push my departure back a few days. The attendant snorted loudly into my ear. 'All flights to New York are booked for the next two weeks,' she said. An icy tendril of fear began to worm through my stomach, but I held panic at bay. I reeled off alternative options for about twenty minutes before she cut me off for good. 'We have no flights to Cuzco from Chile. And you'll be lucky if you can get to Lima in time for your Friday morning flight home.'

I rushed to the nearest customer service desk and demanded bus information from northern Chile to Cuzco and then to Lima. The bewildered employee tried to keep up with my barrage of questions, but no matter which way I turned the map, the Andes kept getting in the way. 'Not possible,' he said to me sympathetically. 'Cuzco's not so far away, but it takes longer than four days to get up and down all those mountains by bus.'

The Calama express pulled in at that moment. I plopped into the first empty seat, put my head down and began to sob quietly into my sweatshirt. My physical exhaustion no doubt contributed to the dramatic reaction, but the bitter disappointment was very real. I'd borrowed money from friends with no idea of when I'd be able to pay it back, and even turned down a few writing assignments to take this trip. Now I was very likely going to miss out on what I had most wanted to see. In between gasps I vehemently cursed my stupidity.

A good night of blissful sea-level sleep rejuvenated me, and I was out and about first thing Monday morning looking for solutions. My friends were clearly dubious, but nonetheless handed over their credit cards and made for a laundrette. I staked out a nearby travel agency. Three hours later, I triumphantly joined them at our hotel, where they were enjoying a sumptuous meal on the patio. I sat down and began shovelling in big bites of *ceviche*, filling them in on my latest plan all the while.

'We leave tonight on an overnight bus to Arica, near the border,' I explained. 'We arrive around seven tomorrow morning. I grab a taxi to Tacna, just over the border in Peru. From there, I go to this address,' I waved the piece of paper given to me by the travel agent, 'and I get my plane tickets. From Tacna I fly to Arequipa and spend the night there. Wednesday morning I fly to Cuzco. I have the day to go to Macchu Picchu and Thursday morning I fly from Cuzco to Lima. I spend an evening in Lima and catch my scheduled flight to New York Friday morning.' I grinned reassuringly as I said this, trying to convince them and myself that things would actually go so smoothly. The lack of tickets didn't help; for some reason, the travel agent could bill them in her office but not issue them and I had to be in Tacna to pick them all up before noon. Furthermore, I'd gotten the last available seats on most of the flights – there was absolutely no wiggle room at all. I was putting on a brave front, but it made me exceedingly nervous.

Lauren squirmed ominously in her chair. 'Macchu Picchu is four hours away from Cuzco by train,' she said, 'and your flight doesn't arrive until 9 a.m.'

I knew from her expression she was trying to tell me something very bad without actually saying it. I swallowed a morsel of fish, took a swig of beer and replied, 'Yeah, and –?'

She surveyed me with her big blues eyes for what seemed like ages. 'The last train to Macchu Picchu leaves the Cuzco station at 8.30.'

Beer bottles flew everywhere as I lunged for the guidebook. My disbelieving bleats changed to moans of acceptance upon seeing it in black and white. Sensing a total meltdown, everyone got busy. Lauren scrambled for details on helicopter fares while Rick grabbed more beer. But it was Rich who saved my sanity. 'Why not try the Web?' he suggested.

I rushed to a nearby Internet café and did a frantic Google search. Up popped the web page of Sky Viajes, based in Cuzco and specialising in trips to Macchu Picchu. Luckily the café also offered phone service. I gave the clerk my number and waited impatiently for the connection to be put through.

'*Buenos días,*' said a voice. It sounded good – smooth, confident, very professional. I took a deep breath and asked who was speaking.

'Jorge Cornejo,' came the reply.

'*Bueno*, Jorge,' I said. 'I need your help.' He listened quietly and with intense concentration. When I finished there was a moment's pause and then he said regretfully, 'No, *niña*, I'm sorry. It can't be done.'

My knuckles whitened as I gripped the receiver. I didn't have much energy left and I knew if Jorge turned me down I'd give up entirely. Squeezing my eyes shut I made one last impassioned plea.

A gentle sigh wafted through the phone. 'Okay,' I heard. 'Let me talk to some people.' An hour later he called back, fully committed to the cause.

'You will throw away everything that is non-essential. Get a small bag that you can carry with you. Do *not* check anything, *entiendes?* You must run off the plane. I will be waiting for you with a driver.'

He paused for a minute, consulted with someone on the other end, then resumed.

'The train to Macchu Picchu stops at Ollantaytambo at 10.05 a.m. It's a 45-minute drive from Cuzco. It's the last stop that's accessible by car. If you follow my directions exactly, and if there are no delays, we should be able to get you there in time to meet the train.'

To this day Lauren insists I knocked several web browsers offline with my hysterical leaping. I shot out of the café and into a department store, where I spent my last few dollars on a small backpack. Then it was back to the hotel to empty my larger bag. A hotel worker delightedly took my abandoned things (she had several family members that were *gordito*, she told me, so my clothes would fit them nicely).

The four of us had a sleepless voyage to Arica and it was a relief to pull into the sparse bus station the next morning and disembark. Lauren slipped a final wad of cash into my hand and I waved goodbye to my friends in the cold, grainy light of dawn. A taxi driver wedged me into a dilapidated station wagon with several other passengers and we set off.

We crossed the remainder of Chile's enormous Atacama Desert in just under an hour, including a twenty-minute wait at the customs office. Before I had time to properly appreciate the reddish morning colours on the sandy landscape, I was being shooed out of the car in Peru. A dashing cab driver with an uncanny resemblance to John Huston pulled up. 'Take me to this address,' I commanded breathlessly. 'I need to pick up some plane tickets urgently.' He read the card with a perplexed air, but dutifully headed into traffic. We meandered aimlessly for about fifteen minutes, then he pulled over. 'Look,' he said, 'this agency isn't in Tacna, it's in Arica. You're in the wrong country.'

That sent me right over the edge. I had just under two hundred dollars in my pocket, half of which was earmarked for Jorge, and no more credit cards. I opened my mouth but nothing came out – questions swarmed through my brain. What the hell had happened? Did I misunderstand the instructions or was it the travel agent who screwed up? What if I couldn't get my tickets before noon but I spent all my money trying? What if I jumped through all these hoops and still didn't make it to Macchu Picchu?

And why, why, why hadn't I planned this out before? For the second time in forty-eight hours, hot tears stung my eyes.

My salvation arrived in the form of Gabriel, a sixtyish Peruvian with a full head of greying hair and a portly belly. He'd innocently pulled over in his cab to say hello to his friend – and inherited me. 'Don't worry,' said John Huston, shifting me to the front seat of Gabriel's sedan. 'He's my friend and he's got the taxi licence to go through customs. He'll help you.'

Gabriel climbed into the driver's seat, handed me a tissue, told me to put on my seatbelt, and did a U-turn. We drove in silence until the border approached on the horizon.

'Don't say anything to the guard,' Gabriel warned. He smiled at the young Peruvian officer, who looked at my passport suspiciously. He delayed us with half an hour of pointless questions but finally waved us through.

For the next two hours Gabriel drove me all over Arica. The first agency didn't have my tickets and sent us to three others before we tracked down everything I needed. By one o'clock that afternoon we were back at the Arica bus station. With everything squared away, Gabriel wanted to ferry more passengers over the border on the return trip.

Later we lunched together at his taxi-driver hangout; he told his friends my plight while I slurped soup. '*Ay, pobrecita,*' they all murmured. Then he drove me to the airport for my evening flight to Arequipa. I tried to give him some money – he'd paid out at least ten dollars in gas and parking. He took a small bill and refused the rest.

'Keep your money, *querida,*' he said to me gently. 'You're going to need it.' He put a piece of paper in my hand and told me he'd made a reservation in my name at an inexpensive hotel in Arequipa. Then he reached out and tapped me lightly on the cheek, an affectionate gesture typical of South America. '*Vaya con Dios,*' he whispered. With that, he disappeared.

Unbelievably, I made it to Arequipa without further incident. A taxi driver named Rambo took me from the airport to my hotel and insisted on doing the reverse trip for me in the morning. 'Don't be late,' I shouted as he pulled away. I checked in, took a shower, set the alarm for 5 a.m., and fell asleep.

There was just enough time for a quick peek at Arequipa's whitewashed streets the next morning before Rambo roared up. He looked horrible, all bloodshot eyes and wild hair, and swerved all over the road. 'Are you drunk?' I demanded. No, he replied, it was a question of avoiding rocks. 'What rocks?' I cried.

Luck seemed to be against me again. Angry over hikes in bus fares, Peruvians had peppered the roads with small boulders. Rambo waited until we reached a stoplight before turning to inform me that the airport runway would be covered as well. 'Your flight won't be going anywhere this morning,' he said pessimistically.

There was a small delay while workers cleared the tarmac, but we landed in Cuzco only fifteen minutes late. I bolted out of the cabin, tore through the main terminal and came to a screeching halt outside the front doors. It was chaos – people hawking hotels, souvenirs, woven goods and crafts. The din overwhelmed me. Where was I supposed to go?

As I turned this way and that, a booming voice called my name. Seconds later a powerful man in a dark suit had wrestled me out of the throng.

It was Jorge. 'Give me your bag and your tickets to Lima and New York,' he ordered. 'I will confirm your remaining flights and leave your things in your hotel room. Everything you need for today is in this packet. Now go with Julio!'

Even as my mind rebelled against turning my bag over to a stranger, my feet were obediently padding after Julio, a slight and handsome young man. We jumped into his tiny red car and squealed out of the airport.

Julio kept up a running patter as we careened down the switch-back trail that passed for the road. His hand tapped the horn incessantly and once we almost eradicated an entire flock of sheep. Deep, unforgiving chasms loomed on either side of us. After two near misses with oncoming lorries, I declared a moratorium on chitchat until we reached the bottom. We made it down one side of the Sacred Valley of the Incas in slightly more than thirty minutes and as we rounded the final turn, Julio started laughing like a loon.

'I am sorry for you but I must go faster,' he said happily. 'It is now almost ten o'clock. Ollantaytambo is just across the valley bottom. At this rate we will be there in fifteen minutes. But the train will be there in five.'

Bile filled my mouth. 'Would you mind turning your head to see if the train is coming out of the mountains behind us?' Julio asked. He said everything with such charm that the implications always took a moment to register.

Only then did I notice that the road ran parallel to a set of railroad tracks. I craned my neck around and for a moment thought we were safe. Then I saw it: a small plume of smoke growing steadily larger as the train steamed along rapidly in our wake.

In a flash I forgot about throwing up. I even forgot about dying. 'It's coming, Julio!' I screamed. 'It's going to beat us.' The car shimmered violently but, as though alive to my need, unbelievably spurted faster as he shifted gears and put his foot all the way down. The train flew by just as we started up the small incline into the village square. Julio's eyes narrowed to concentrated pinpoints. 'Be ready to run,' he hissed between clenched teeth.

He squeezed the car through two stone columns, executed a 180-degree turn which sprayed gravel and cackling chickens everywhere, and pushed me out of the car. I fell on my backpack but was up and running toward the closed entrance gate in seconds. It was blocked by villagers hoping to get on the train to sell their wares to tourists, and two stone-faced, machine-gun wielding guards who stood in front of it.

'Show your ticket,' I heard Julio say from behind me. I caught the younger guard's eyes and waved the packet Jorge had given me earlier. He cleared a path for me using the butt of his gun. '*Pasa*,' he said.

I squeezed through the chicken wire and in five quick strides was on the running board of the train. It shuddered beneath my feet and began to move, but I was firmly planted. Panting, I turned to give Julio a victory wave. He was pinched between the guards, hopping up and down and yelling frantically. The train was gathering momentum and rapidly gaining distance from the station. As the last blast of the whistle faded away, his words floated toward me. 'Ginger,' I heard. 'You must find Mr Willy!'

'Whatever,' I said to myself, even as I nodded comprehendingly. I was in no mood to go chasing down some mysterious Willy talisman. All I wanted was to reach the ancient site in one piece, find a quiet corner and curl up in the weak Peruvian winter sun. In short order, I found myself doing exactly that. The silence and splendour of Macchu Picchu filled me completely and my thoughts drifted peacefully between past and present. Suddenly a short man with strong Indian features appeared in front of me. He unabashedly took a good long look, tilting his head sideways and flashing strong white teeth in the sun. My heart thumped once, heavily, and then I knew. 'Hello,' I said, with some resignation. 'You must be Mr Willy.'

And indeed he was – Mr Willy, tour guide extraordinaire. He marched me all over the site, talking nonstop about the marvellous mysteries of the Incan Empire. He spent four enthralling hours teaching me everything he knew, and gradually the tension of the last few days ebbed completely away. I'd become so fixated on just getting to Macchu Picchu that I almost forgot my long-held fascination with the place – luckily Mr Willy was there to remind me. The train ride back to Cuzco was anticlimatic, but seldom have I felt such undiluted joy. My bag was waiting in my hotel room as promised, with passport, plane tickets and wallet intact. Later I toted up the day's price tag and found that Jorge had only charged me for basic expenses (how he compensated Julio for risking his life I can't imagine). I was astounded that neither Gabriel nor Jorge had attempted to price-gouge me in my moment of need. The thin woollen blanket on my bed didn't do much to keep out the cold, but I fell soundly asleep, warmed by all my friends' generosity. Two days later I was on my way back to New York, empty in the pocket but loaded with the richness of life.

Egg Child

SARAH LEVIN

Sarah Levin is originally from the US East Coast but moved to Alaska after she graduated from Wesleyan University in 2001. She is a violinist and freelance writer, and enjoys running sled dogs and clambering over glaciers when she can. In addition to her semester abroad in Tanzania, she has travelled in Europe, the Middle East and South America, finding herself in countless humbling situations along the way. This is her first book publication.

WHEN I WOKE UP it was still dark and I thought I was in the bowels of a ghost. My mosquito net hung loosely over the bed, white and gauzy and full of holes. I slapped a hand to my temple to crush a mosquito that had found an entrance, and slowly raked my fingernails over the row of bedbug bites on my elbow.

The equatorial heat, even at five in the morning, had settled over my limbs like moist candyfloss. I could hear the call to prayer being broadcast over loudspeakers in the mosque down the road, haunting and lovely Arabic words sounding brassy over the anti-quated system. I shuffled to the bathroom in my flip-flops, sat on the toilet and put my face in my hands. Yesterday the doctor had said that my stomach lining was coming out, that I should take it easy. Today I could not take it easy.

Downstairs in the dining room, the kitchen staff was setting out a thermos of tea and bowls of sugar. Their brown faces were sleepy, quiet and smiling. One of the women came over with a mug and a piece of lemon. She touched my hair and said, You will be better. Have a good journey.

I had made this trip several times before. I was living in a wildlife refuge, monitoring the animals for parasites, and had to come into town every few days to use the veterinarian's micro-scope. As the crow flies it may have been one hundred kilometres back to the refuge, but it would be five hours or more before I would see my tent. I took three tablets of Loperamide as I waited by the roadside for a minibus. They chugged along the road in droves, the drivers' faces looking hard and stern, the slim young boys who collected the fares slapping the side of the vans with cal-lused hands. One slap meant a pick-up, two a drop-off. I lifted my arm and a van careened to the side of the road. The boy who opened the door was wearing a New York Yankees baseball cap. He grinned at me with brown-stained teeth and yammered in Swahili, and all I could catch was 'white lady'.

Pulling my scarf tightly around my head, I worked my way into the van. There was no room to sit, so I hunched over and grabbed onto the back of a seat, accidentally yanking on a young girl's hair as we rolled over a pothole. She turned and smiled gently, took the bag I was holding and nestled it in her kilt-clad lap as we braced ourselves for the next lurch.

The bus station was teeming with merchants selling bottles of orange-pink juice, rows of biscuits, tired battery-powered stereos and used T-shirts. Ticket-sellers crowded around me, yelping East African destinations in rapid succession: 'Nairobi!' 'Tanga!' 'Dar es Salaam!' Buses groaned into motion, spewing brown gobs of exhaust; men ran after them, hitting the sides, leaping into the doorways as they took off down the narrow streets. I muscled myself into a minibus bound for Moshi and looked into the horde of dark faces that had almost simultaneously turned to stare at the white girl. A pain seized my stomach and I breathlessly slipped between two elderly women, willing the Loperamide to soothe my intestines.

The bus grew more crowded. A toddler was deposited on my lap, my shoulders squeezed between the two soft women beside me. They spoke to me in slow, easy Swahili, asking where I was from and where I was going. They touched their hands to mine, and we swayed together on the long road.

The women waved, imitating my gesture, when I got off at the stand in the town of Boma ya Ngombe. The merchants again surrounded me, more desperate this time, because there were never white faces here. I shook my head slowly, over and over, glancing through their bony forms for the next bus. The wait here was never longer than five minutes, though the ride was more cramped. I was pulled on, prodded towards the window across from a man holding a chicken by the legs. The bird squawked, its eyes beady, its white feathers brushing my fingertips in a frenzied escape attempt.

It was past noon; sunlight poured through the glass like untouchable fire. I wiped the sweat from my eyebrows. My teeth chattered. The man across from me watched with bloodshot eyes, his chicken trembling on his knees.

At Sanya Juu I crawled over seven laps, the plastic bags tied to my wrists trailing behind me. The sun had disappeared by now, its yellow beams shrouded in clouds. I dodged a puddle and headed toward a small kiosk by the side of the road. I asked to use a bathroom; the woman pointed behind me to a guesthouse. Crossing the road, I was met with the upturned glances of children, their dusty bellies poking out beneath too-small shirts. One boy took my hand as I crossed. His feet were bare, as wrinkled as a forty-year-old's. His hand was moist in the heat and warmed my own.

The men outside the guesthouse dropped their voices as I approached. I was shaking so badly that the bags on my wrists were rustling and the men looked up expectantly. I greeted them with a bowed head. A woman carrying a large bucket of laundry on her head took my hand and showed me down a narrow corridor to the bathroom, a dark closet with a hole thirty centimetres in diameter leading into a deep pit of excrement. I could hear the rats. The men and women outside could hear me. They could hear the sickness they all had endured so many times before rushing into that pit, and they had a bottle of warm soda waiting for me when I finished. I could barely manage to thank them, my face so burned with feverish shame.

The pick-up truck was laden with bags of maize and cabbage and four other passengers. I tiptoed gingerly around them and perched myself in a corner on top of a burlap sack. I tightened my scarf over my head to shield from the wind, which was blowing westward from Mount Kilimanjaro. On a clear day I would have been able to see the long, white expanse of the summit casting its shadow on the montane forest of the lower slopes, but today those slopes were whisked away into the clouds, and everything was the same dull grey. The truck's engine and I shuddered in unison as we prepared to leave.

But we weren't leaving. We moved three metres forward and stopped while two more passengers, maybe brothers, hoisted themselves into the pile of vegetables. They had long scars careening across both cheekbones and were carrying handfuls of oranges. They did not speak to anyone or look at anyone, just stared down at the stagnant pools of water in the road.

The rain started, tiny flecks of rain that seemed to boil and freeze at the same time on my skin. I opened one of my plastic bags and emptied the contents – two T-shirts and my toothbrush – onto my skirt and placed the bag over my head. The other riders watched curiously. The boys with the scars smiled stained-tooth smiles, sympathetic, amused.

After the driver had poured a jug of petrol into the tank he jogged toward one of the kiosks by the road and then disappeared. I glanced at my watch; it was getting late. In the sky I could see a stretch of sunlight between the dripping clouds, mustard-coloured instead of the white gold that had streamed down in arcs earlier.

Several minutes later the driver emerged from the kiosk and settled into the truck, revving the engine. The road, though full of potholes, resembled concrete and inspired the driver, who zipped across it and made sudden shifts in direction to avoid larger ditches. The concrete soon ended and dark, packed dirt stretched ahead, sandwiched between endless green-and-yellow fields. I focussed my eyes on a bag of maize and bit my tongue. I held my face up to the rain to cool my skin. The taller boy holding oranges asked if I was sick.

Just a little, I said.

White people are always sick, he said. I think you must be fragile, an egg child.

The village of Ngare Nairobi came into view forty-five minutes later; we slowed for a herd of cattle and sheep crossing the road. The villagers followed the vehicle with their eyes and the children ran after us, shrieking greetings.

I slid off the back of the truck, pushing the damp sleeves of my sweater to my elbows. As soon as my feet touched the ground they sank deep into mud. It was sticky and cold, and moulded to my skin. As I pulled, straining my calves, my flip-flops slipped off. I stood on a drier patch of the road, looking at the bright red rubber half-buried in the mud, and felt a stone in my throat.

I awkwardly brought my skirt to my knees and bent down, reaching toward the mess, when the brothers with the oranges stepped beside me. The taller one yanked on the shoes and held them out to me.

For the egg child, he said. And have this, for your journey.

He handed me an orange and took his brother's hand as they walked away.

It would be a walk of nearly two hours back to my camp, and the sun was quickly dropping towards the horizon behind the clouds. There was no latrine here so I went behind a tree and due to a lack of tissues used leaves instead. I slipped all of my extra clothes on, but my sweater was still damp and the chills would not subside.

The village disappeared behind me. Far to the horizon I could see only trees and long stretches of savanna. I walked by several tilting houses with tin roofs, chickens in the yards, bare-bottomed toddlers. The hem of my skirt faded from white into dusky brown and finally black; the women passing by had no mud on their clothes and looked as though they had just awoken from a refreshing sleep. Even their feet appeared to glide over the mud. They seemed to wonder about me, this slovenly, pale figure.

I would not make it before dark. I hadn't brought a flashlight. I wondered what I would do, and then I vomited into the bushes.

As I stood and watched the sky darkening, I heard the rusty wheels of a bicycle come to a halt behind me. The boy was my age, it seemed, and skin and bones. He asked where I had come from and where I was going. I wiped my mouth and motioned to a distant cluster of Jacaranda trees with a frantic hand.

It is too far a walk, he said. I will take you there.

He took the bags from my wrists. As he knotted them over the handlebars, I could see the tendons on his forearms and a glistening in his face. His shirt was tattered and one of his flip-flops had a broken strap. He was still for a moment, looking at the sky as rain started to fall again, and then held his arm out to help me climb onto the bumper.

As I teetered on the back of his bicycle, the boy pedalled on, breathing hard with the extra weight. I grabbed hold of the seat with one hand and steadied myself with my other hand on his back. His vertebrae felt like stepping stones.

Serendipity

LAURA FRASER

Laura Fraser is a freelance writer who lives in San Francisco. Her latest book, *An Italian Affair*, a travel memoir, was a US bestseller. She is currently writing for *Organic Style*, *Gourmet* and *Mother Jones*, and is working on a novel.

I AM NOT RELIGIOUS, at least not in any established way. I do believe that the universe offers up mysterious signs and synchronicities though. And, like a lot of travellers, I'm susceptible to those signs, forever seeking clues to direct me towards extraordinary locations and experiences that aren't listed in guidebooks. Perhaps what I'm looking for when I travel is spiritual. But whether the signs I seek are cosmic or mere coincidence, I certainly don't attribute them to anything I learned about in Sunday school.

Still, when I was travelling around Israel several years ago, there was something about the Sea of Galilee that beckoned me. In Israel, the Sea of Galilee is just a lake – the Kinneret. But any place that is overflowing with history and myth, spiritual teachings and prophecies – and is Mary Magdalene's birthplace to boot – is worth exploring, and probably full of mysterious mojo.

I visited the Sea of Galilee one September, stopping in a town called Tiberias. I plunged into the lake right away, and the waters were warm and refreshing. But after the swim, I still felt I wanted to somehow immerse myself deeper in the mythological sea. Maybe having grown up with tales of Jesus walking on the water, I wanted to go out to the middle of the sea and test the surface.

So I decided to take a boat across the lake. There wasn't a cheap ferry service from Tiberias to the other side, Ein Gev, and as a backpacker, I had no funds to hire a boat. But as I was casting about for a ride I saw a boat, loaded with people on organised tours, getting ready to push away from shore. I climbed aboard and took a seat among the tourists on one of the benches. In no time we were chugging along, and I was enjoying the fresh breeze, the water, and the view of the Golan Heights beyond. I thought it would take only half an hour or so to make it to the other side – not enough time for anyone to notice an interloper or make a fuss. There was more than one tour group, so the Baptists could just assume I was with the Pentecostals, and vice versa.

Then we stopped in the middle of the lake. The passengers brought out their video cameras to record the spot where Jesus

161

apparently walked on water, and a few threw candy wrappers overboard. I dipped my hand in and the water felt just like water. I thought we'd get going again soon, but a minister in flowing robes came to the bow, and I realised we were in for a full-blown church service. The benches had turned into pews, and there was no slipping out the side door. There was going to be plenty of time for whoever was in charge to realise that I wasn't one of the retired pilgrims on tour, but a stowaway.

So I prayed. Not literally – well, maybe a tiny bit– but I bowed my head to feign religious fervour, so no one would see or bother me. When the sermon finally ended, about an hour and a half later, my Sunday-school training came in handy, because I could chime in on 'Michael, Row the Boat Ashore' and several other hymns. Some of the passengers, in matching ecumenical fish T-shirts, were eyeing me sceptically, but when I sang those 'hallelujahs', they nodded piously and turned the other way. When the boat finally did make its way ashore, I bounded off, and no one ever questioned me.

On the banks, I watched as the tourist groups filed into their special buses to resume their itinerary. We hadn't stopped at Ein Gev, where I thought I could catch a bus back to the youth hostel. We hadn't stopped in a town at all. We were in the middle of nowhere. I wasn't about to push my luck climbing aboard the bus with the tourists again. But I had no map, hardly any money – I'd left that back at the hostel – and only my swimsuit in a little bag. I glanced at the lake, easily fifteen kilometres across. Not even Jesus could walk that far.

There was nothing to do but hitchhike. Since no cars came along the deserted road, I started walking in what I assumed was the shortest direction around the lake back to my youth hostel. With a full day ahead of me, I could walk the whole way if need be. But after about an hour a battered jeep pulled up, and a weather-beaten Israeli asked me if I needed a ride. I hesitated but climbed in, and he asked me where I was going. Tiberias, I said, and he nodded. 'But this side of the lake is so much more beautiful,' he said.

He began describing the wonders of the area, exuberantly pointing here and there, and asked whether I liked waterfalls.

Who doesn't? And how fortunate that the universe had dropped a local guide in my path just when I needed one. I was game for adventure – that's why I was travelling. The man, a leathery fisherman in his forties, drove me to a secret waterfall cascading through some cliffs, surrounded by carob trees. Then he picked a grapefruit and offered me some breakfast. He told me he went out fishing when it was dark, as was the custom on the Kinneret, and roamed around during the day, just appreciating nature. His days were unplanned; his only aim to find a beautiful spot to visit, or an unexpected companion. Even though I was the traveller, he was the one, it seemed, who was leading the life of exploration and serendipity, living from one chance encounter to the next. When he asked if I wanted to travel along with him for awhile, I told him sure – as long as he was going in my direction.

He smiled. 'But you're lost.'

The fisherman turned his jeep onto some rough side roads, telling me, in his scrappy English, about his time living in New York City – a place that couldn't have seemed farther away. He stopped at what he said was the old Syrian Officers' Club – abandoned baths where pure, clean, warm mineral water poured into an old stone swimming pool. I changed into my swimsuit while he made a fire for coffee. I had a luxurious swim and then the best coffee I'd ever tasted.

'Why do you trust me to take you to these places?' the fisherman asked me, lighting a hand-rolled cigarette. I suddenly felt chilled in my swimsuit, and wrapped my shirt around me. These days I would answer, 'Because I was stupid.' But then I felt invulnerable, protected by some combination of American feminism, naiveté and my own intuition.

'I can sense when someone is trustworthy,' I told him, hoping I was right. 'You're obviously not the sort of person who would ever take advantage of anyone.'

He chuckled and then sighed.

We jeeped around some more, leaving the lush officers' oasis to bounce along an old army road littered with crushed metal carcasses of war vehicles, a landscape still devastated from the war with Syria. 'Were you in the war?' I asked.

'Yes,' he said curtly. 'You Americans don't know anything about war.'

We drove to a path and hiked up through another lush cluster of greenery to a pond cut in rock by a stream. The sides of the pond were sheer hexagonal columns, and the pond was hexagonal too. An amazing spot. I was glad there were other people at the pool. The atmosphere with the fisherman was no longer so light.

The fisherman took a loaf of bread out of his pocket and tore off a piece. He didn't offer me any. He drove me back to near where he'd picked me up. He hopped out of the jeep, wandered over to a stone building and introduced me to a couple of priests inside. They lived there on the shores of the Kinneret, at the church, he explained, where Jesus made Saint Peter the first pope. The priests wore grimy sweatshirts under their frocks, and were drinking beer. They passed around more beers, joking about their hardship post by the beach.

After some time with the priests, who seemed more like construction workers in costume, I mentioned I had to get back to my youth hostel. The fisherman said he'd drive me, he was going that way anyway. The priests drunkenly nodded along, approvingly, and secure with their blessings, I got back in the jeep with the fisherman. After travelling a few kilometres from the priests' lair, he slowed the jeep, put his hand on my leg and said he was taking me to his place. 'Thanks,' I told him, 'I'm staying at the hostel.' He braked abruptly. 'No,' he said. 'Now it's your turn to pay me back.' Suddenly, I realised, the universe wasn't taking care of me. I laughed at him like it was all a joke between friends. I knew there was no one who was going to come looking for me if I didn't show up at the youth hostel. No one had any idea where I was. I was entirely at this fisherman's mercy.

'I'm sorry,' I said. 'I really have to go back.' I put my hand on the door handle. 'Thanks for showing me so many beautiful places.' I opened the door.

He reached over, put his palm on my breast, and shoved me out the door.

'Go,' he said, and the jeep lurched away.

Stunned, I picked myself up off the ground. I suppose I was lucky. But I was back on the deserted road, and now it was dark. Whatever spiritual shroud of protection I'd supposedly wrapped myself in all day was gone, and I was cold.

I began to panic. I didn't know how to get back, and I didn't want to hitchhike again. I had been teetering on the edge between free-spirited adventure and self-induced danger all day long, and perhaps for months. I was lucky to be left alone, but I wanted a warm bunk in a hostel full of fellow backpackers, and it was far away. For the second time that day, I prayed. Just in case it worked. Here on the shores where all the big miracles of Christianity took place – the loaves and fishes and all – I just wanted a car with a nice couple of religious sightseers who would take me back to my youth hostel.

After about an hour, walking without any sense of direction just to stay warm, I saw headlights off in the distance. I stuck out my thumb. Miraculously the car – a new red rental sedan – stopped. I asked the driver a few questions before I got in. He was an American real-estate agent from Southern California named Larry. He was an ordinary guy in a polo shirt with a stack of guidebooks on the seat beside him. I have never been so happy to see an Orange County realtor in my life.

As Larry drove me back around the lake, I recounted my day to him. He seemed envious of my adventures – not only of the wild day, but of my months of travelling. He was travelling, too, seeing the sights, checking them off one by one on his itinerary. He offered me dinner, and I demurred – I had taken men up on too many offers that day. He insisted and said it was his treat, he just wanted some company. Plus, he said, it looked like I could use a good, warm meal. We went to a restaurant where we ate

Saint Peter's fish and drank wine, all the while sitting next to a group of tourists. It wasn't until I'd almost finished my meal that I realised they were the same tourists who had been on the boat that morning, which seemed like a month ago. I laughed with the warmth of the wine, safe with my memory of the day.

I was grateful to Larry for the comfort, safety and ordinariness he brought to my travels, coming along exactly when I needed him. I sized him up as a fairly dull guy – adventuresome enough to take a month out of his life to travel to a foreign country, but not enough to do anything out of the ordinary when he got there. He was thin, in his mid-thirties, Jewish, alone. He wanted to travel in Israel because it felt familiar, but wasn't sure about going anywhere else. I was the first person he'd had a meal with in days. He was considering returning home early.

'Just keep travelling,' I urged him. He had come all this way, why not keep exploring? Take a boat to Greece, to Italy, to Cyprus. The whole Mediterranean, with all its riches, its art, its history, was at his feet. When in his life would he ever have the chance to do it again? He'd be home, he'd have a job, he'd never get the time off again, except maybe two weeks a year . . .

'Yes,' he said, studying me. 'You're right. Thanks.'

He dropped me off at my youth hostel just before curfew, and I couldn't thank him enough for taking care of me. I berated myself silently at the same time for having put myself in the position where I needed his help, when I'd had to rely on prayer and stupid luck.

I ended up staying in Israel all winter – Israel was relatively peaceful then, in spite of all the machine guns – working as a volunteer on a kibbutz, mainly fishing. Then I made my way down the Sinai Peninsula, spent a month in Egypt, flew to Italy, and travelled in Austria, Hungary and then back to Italy. I was seeing Rome – a city I would come to love – for the first time, and stood in the Pantheon surveying the ceiling. I was overwhelmed with the beauty of the place when I heard someone call my name.

I turned, but didn't see anyone. It must have been someone else; Italy is full of Lauras. Then I heard it again, closer.

'It *is* you,' the voice said. 'Your hair is shorter and it's red.' I had no idea who this hippie-looking guy was – he had scruffy curls, a frayed army jacket and boots. I searched his face.

'Larry,' I said. The Southern California realtor. He smiled.

'Amazing,' he said. 'I barely recognised you.' Same here.

We were both made speechless by the coincidence of meeting up with each other again, five months and five countries apart. Maybe it meant something.

We walked around Rome and sat by the Trevi Fountain, eating hazelnut gelato and recounting our travels. He had taken my advice and continued travelling. After Israel, he'd been island-hopping in Greece. He looked nothing like the stiff, well-scrubbed guy who had picked me up in the rental car. He was tanned, tattered and relaxed. Our coincidence gave us a kind of intimacy together right away. He was hoping, he confessed, to find someone to fall in love with while he was travelling. All the places he'd been had seemed so romantic, except that he was alone. Which made them almost unbearable.

I knew exactly how he felt.

'I'm so glad to run into you,' he said.

We had dinner in a small, cheap place; crispy-crusted pizzas with beer. After a few drinks, he held my hand across the table. I thought to myself, what a great story I could tell about how we met.

Larry walked me to the bus stop to find my way back to my *pensione*, and we made plans to see the Vatican the next day. He mentioned that he wanted to get there half an hour before it opened, so we would meet in front.

The next morning, I arrived a few minutes late. He was happy to see me but kept looking at his watch. I suggested we go have a coffee together before embarking on the Vatican. We were, after all, in Italy and there was no rush. But he wanted to get started.

I was excited to see the Vatican Museum, but I was sure that it would hold none of the mystery of Galilee; it was steeped in religion and history, but it was all labelled, contained, behind glass.

There are three or four guided routes through the Vatican Museum, depending on your museum temperament. You can make a beeline for the Sistine Chapel, or you can study each piece of Etruscan pottery. I am a museum dilettante; I wander in, look at whatever captures my fancy, ignore a lot of Madonnas, and speed past mediaeval armour. Larry had a completely different style. He insisted on stopping in front of each gold coin to understand its origin, reading aloud from his guidebook. After three hours, nowhere close to the Sistine Chapel, I was exasperated. Underneath his romantic exterior, I could see the meticulous Orange County realtor shining through.

We had a late lunch after we finally made it out the gilded portals of the Vatican. Larry tried to order in Italian, but his accent was atrocious. If fate was putting this man into my future, I was going to have a lot of secret cringing to do.

I wanted to order spaghetti with black squid ink. Larry thought that sounded weird and disgusting. He wanted to eat something 'normal'. He also thought that if he had wine with lunch, he wouldn't be alert enough to take in the church with the Caravaggios later that afternoon. He asked for a Coke.

Over my *spaghetti al nero di seppia* and *vino tinto*, I realised that it had been a marvellous coincidence to run into this man who had rescued me, but the coincidence didn't mean anything. I had been travelling for so many months searching for something – hoping that the ever-changing landscapes, languages and people would give me a clue about my life, tell me what direction to go in next. But while I had discovered a great deal about my capacity for independence, and for handling whatever obstacles I encountered, I'd actually had no reliable signs or divine revelations. There was so much to appreciate and experience, but the signs I needed to follow actually came from within.

We finished up lunch. Larry could tell that the romance of our meeting had faded. When I mentioned that I was catching a train that evening to visit my cousin in Florence, he realised that whatever he had thought he had found in me was slipping out of his grasp. He seemed depressed, almost ready to cry. I knew enough about Larry to know that he rarely let himself feel that much.

This time I reached over and held his hand. I told him that he had been incredibly helpful to me in Israel; he'd saved me from a truly bad situation, and I'd always appreciate his kindness. I said I couldn't believe how much he'd changed in those months, how much more adventuresome he seemed. 'I can tell,' I said, 'that you're about to have a really great romantic adventure.'

Larry brightened a little. 'How do you know?' he asked.

I shrugged. 'You're open to it,' I said. 'You found me, which is an incredible coincidence. It's a sign.' I squeezed his hand and let go. We parted outside the restaurant, without exchanging addresses. I wished him luck.

I continued travelling. I spent a few more days in Italy and then took a train to Spain where, finally, I could speak the language. After about a month in Spain I landed in Seville, just in time for the Feria de Sevilla, the big fair where Spaniards parade their magnificent horses during the day and dance flamenco all night long in little *casita* tents set up on the fairgrounds.

One afternoon, after just waking up from sleeping off another long night of dancing, I headed to the fairgrounds to watch the parade of horses. There was an enormous crowd. I looked across the street, my gaze settling on a figure in a worn green jacket that seemed familiar. I must have been tired from dancing all night, because I surely didn't know anyone in Seville. I stared at the man and realised he was staring back at me.

It was Larry.

We just looked at each other for a minute, not believing our eyes. Then a woman tugged at his arm. He waved at me, and I just waved back.

It was an outrageous coincidence to see him again, but I knew it was just coincidence. Still, I interpreted it as a sign. After having travelled for nine months, searching for a place or person to give my life meaning, I decided it was time to go home. It was time to become the person I was searching for in my travels, in all those signs.

Arab Music

JENNIE ROTHENBERG

Jennie Rothenberg began travelling at the age of four months, when her parents took her to France for a six-week course with the Indian teacher Maharishi Mahesh Yogi. Her favourite spots in the world include the northern coast of California, the tip of South Africa, the Alpine Mountains surrounding Lake Lucerne and the sky above Fairfield, Iowa. She has written for the *Chicago Tribune* and is an ongoing contributor to the *Atlantic Monthly* online.

I HEARD THE MUSIC that first night, at two in the morning as we drove up the hillside. It hadn't rained for three months and the air itself seemed to be sleeping. There were no crickets chirping, no locusts humming. When we turned off the engine, the only sound was the pop of the trunk and then Allon's footsteps as he went to rummage for his sleeping bag. His girlfriend Nimrah, a thin Yemenite Jew with bead-laced dreadlocks, hauled out the tent she'd brought from her mother's house. I stood a distance away from them, just making out the shape of the landscape against the background of stars. The hills were immense here, almost mountains, and in the morning I would see they were covered with olive trees. But tonight I noticed only the clusters of lights – and the sound of far-off music.

'Where's that singing coming from?' I called to the others.

Allon lifted his head. 'It's coming up from the valley. All those lights down there are Arab villages.' Listening closely, I could just make out the distinctive Middle Eastern warble and what sounded like drums or clapping.

It was July 1999, a peaceful time in Israel. Nobody died that summer, or if they did, it was from sickness, accidents or old age. People spent their days at the beach in Tel Aviv eating *glida*, rich gelato-like ice cream. They wandered through markets, bargaining with Sephardic vendors for handmade leather sandals. In the Old City, Arab boys lay in the courtyard outside the mosque, heads in their mothers' laps. A deep contentment flowed like sap, and it was hard to imagine anything coming to disturb that feeling.

I was in Israel because it seemed like a good summer to travel, and because I had some sixty relatives scattered throughout that small country. I also had Allon, a college friend who had insisted on hosting me for the first few days. He was a skinny boy who carried himself like a true Israeli, walking briskly with his head held high. I'd been in the country only a few hours when he announced that we'd be leaving Tel Aviv at midnight for the Galilee.

Our campsite was at the edge of a little town called Harrarit, the only Jewish community for miles around. Allon had many friends there, and the next morning a friend of his named P'ninah invited us over for breakfast. The view from her kitchen window swept down the bright hills toward the Arab villages below. I asked P'ninah about her neighbours in the valley. 'Sure, we have many Arab friends,' she replied, cutting slices of bread for her two small girls. 'You have to remember, the Arabs in the Galilee are Israeli citizens. They speak Hebrew and work with Jews every day.'

'Harrarit people all buy their vegetables in the Arab markets,' Allon added.

'You can take her there, Allon,' P'ninah suggested. 'Why don't you call Motlak?'

'That's a good idea,' he agreed, stretching out his long legs. 'But don't tell her anything. Just let her see.'

After breakfast, we were in Allon's car again. Nimrah put on some loud music and Allon drove quickly, too quickly, down the steep, winding road. The greedy light seemed to swallow all colour, leaving bleached terrain and pale blue sky. Looking out the window, I saw all I hadn't been able to see the night before. Rows of gnarled olive trees spread out like a quilt in all directions, and the valleys were dotted with cube-shaped white houses.

We dipped into a narrow street lined with Arabic signs. Many buildings looked only half finished, but their arched windows gave them an odd note of elegance. An old woman sat at the side of the road, and I could tell from the bobbing of her head that she was singing.

When Allon pulled into a dusty driveway, a moustached man came around a corner to greet us. '*Shalom*,' he welcomed Allon, slapping him warmly on the back. 'I, Motlak,' he announced to me. 'I speak English . . . fifty-fifty.'

Entering the courtyard, I saw that Allon had made a 'reservation' at a sort of restaurant where we were the only guests. A woman, introduced as Motlak's wife, was setting the table with curved white dishes. A pool of oil lay atop the paprika-flecked hummus, and there were several bowls of olives, both green and

brown. We used freshly baked flatbreads to scoop up the egg-
plant, okra and a sour substance called *lebne*. Vines twisted
overhead, and peering upwards, I saw that they were hanging
with green grapes and pink flowers.

After the meal, Motlak reappeared and led us into a cool, dark
room. All kinds of ornaments decorated the stone walls: long
robes, coloured lamps, musical instruments. Our host motioned
to a wooden bench strewn with colourful pillows. '*Bavakasha*,' he
said in Hebrew. 'Please. Sit.'

Something on a low tabletop caught Nimrah's eye. 'Allon,' she
whispered, 'a *nargila*!' She grinned at me. 'You can tell everyone
back in America that you smoked one.' I looked suspiciously at
the enormous water pipe. With its tubes and bulbs, it reminded
me of something from a mad scientist's laboratory. Motlak
dropped a sticky square into the top, and a moment later, the
glass filled with pale brown smoke.

'Come on,' Allon urged me. 'It's only apple-flavoured tobacco.'
But I just watched as Nimrah and Allon lay on the cushions, blowing smoke rings like the caterpillar in *Alice in Wonderland*. Their
posture was supremely relaxed, but their eyes betrayed their giddy
excitement. They were Tel Aviv kids who rarely saw this other side
of Israel. Nimrah lived in an apartment building on a busy street,
and Allon lived in a suburban house with a big swimming pool.

While his guests smoked, Motlak brought out a violin. He
began to play for us, liquid, sliding notes that echoed faintly
against the cave-like walls. As if she'd been called for, a little girl
came shyly into the room holding a drum one-third of her height.
She tapped in time with her father's song, an intricate rhythm that
seemed to move effortlessly through her fingers. I forgot about the
nargila and leaned forward, wholly absorbed in the music.

After the performance, Motlak beamed at my praise. He said
something to Allon in Hebrew. 'You are invited to be a guest of
his family,' Allon translated. 'You can eat supper here and in the
evening they'll show you the whole village. They'll drive you back
to us in the morning.'

The invitation was both frightening and enticing. I opened my mouth to politely decline. Then I looked down at the little girl who was staring at me in wonder. These were Arabs, people who had existed for me only in the troubled lines of black-and-white newsprint. Now here was their world, alive, in full colour and flavour. I doubted whether an opportunity like this would ever come again.

I half expected Allon to dissuade me, but I saw only a well-concealed flicker of surprise as he coolly translated my acceptance. I guessed he was as curious as I was to see how my adventure would turn out. Rising for the door, he kissed my cheek and told me, 'We'll see you in the morning.' Motlak's little daughter led Allon and Nimrah to their car, and a moment later, the engine's sound disappeared into silence. We were alone. Motlak and me.

Motlak brought two small porcelain cups of coffee. 'Drink,' he insisted. It was bitter and strong. He sat on the bench, facing me. 'I speak English . . . fifty-fifty,' he quipped again. I tried out a few words of thanks in Hebrew. He nodded and then said, 'Good. Very good. I . . . love you.'

I pulled back, astonished. Something had obviously been lost in the translation. I let an awkward moment go by and then asked, 'Where will I sleep tonight?'

'*Po*,' he replied. '*V'gam ani po.*' Here. And also me here. To clear up any ambiguity, he raised two fingers and spoke the Hebrew number, '*Shta'im.*'

Looking back, I can never quite understand why I didn't leap to my feet and demand to be brought back to Harrarit. I was as if in an altered state, dazed by the foreign surroundings, bewildered by the surreal, broken Hebrew. If I stopped to think, I would risk coming to my senses and leaving this adventure behind forever.

Four Hebrew words stumbled off my tongue: '*Lo. Rak ani po.*' No. Only me here. Motlak understood. He threw up his hands as if in surrender. 'Okay,' he assured me. '*Kol beseder.*' I told him that

I wanted to spend the day with his children, and he jumped from his seat. When we passed his wife, washing dishes at an outdoor sink, I searched her face for signs of distrust, but her smile seemed genuinely friendly. Whether or not she suspected Motlak's offer, he would not repeat it again.

The sunlight blazed brighter now, merging all the features of the landscape together. Motlak brought me down a steep ladder, through twisted bushes and clouds of loose dust. I started to slip and Motlak stretched out his arm. 'Fifty-fifty,' he joked. 'Fifty-fifty.' I had no choice but to rely on him as he led me down the slope, supporting me with his hand.

We came to a newer house halfway down the hillside. A man in rose-coloured pyjama pants sprawled out on the couch while five children played on the floor around him. 'Welcome to our home,' he said in English that was better than 'fifty-fifty'. 'My brother says you would enjoy to stay here this afternoon.'

A child came over to inspect me, a bright-faced girl wearing a yellow T-shirt with Arabic lettering. The little drummer stood behind her, a blue ribbon tied in her hair. I picked up a crayon and drew a stick figure with a bow on top of its head. Both girls giggled. Passing the paper between us, we drew houses, animals, flowers, trees and the sun that shone outside the large open windows.

Late in the afternoon, Motlak's brother asked if I'd like to take a nap. 'You can rest in the children's room,' he offered kindly. With a smile, his wife handed me a long blue robe and led me to the back of the house, showing me where I could shower and rest.

I awoke two hours later to the sound of children's voices. Wandering outside, I saw the girls sitting on a dusty slope, absorbed in a game of dolls. Neighbours sat all around in folding chairs, eating slices of watermelon and drinking black coffee. The gathering had the air of a holiday, but I knew the scene must have been the same at this time every afternoon. The light slanted from the west, turning the dusty hills and air to gold. Somewhere in the distance a cow mooed. A wind chime tinkled. In the spaces between its notes was an immense, expansive silence.

While the adults drank their coffee, the smallest boy crawled up onto my lap. He was all softness and big eyes. I rested my chin in his hair, listening to the relaxed chatter. A little girl smiled at me, leaning against her father's arm, and I smiled back. She reminded me of my own childhood photographs: same dark hair, same almond eyes. When the boy reached for his mother, a group of girls bounded over and pulled me up, holding onto my hands. Together we half walked, half ran up the road toward Motlak's house, through the hills and the thick sunlight.

In the evening, Motlak's seventeen-year-old son, Alaa, came home from his day's work on a Tiberias cruise ship. He was a tall boy with a heart-shaped face, sleekly handsome like a cat. His English was better than my Hebrew, and once I finished eating, he asked if I'd like to go for a walk. 'I can show you around Dier Hanna,' he said. I realised then that I'd never known what this village was called. I liked the way it sounded, like the name of an old woman.

It was eleven o'clock, but children were still playing and songs came from every courtyard. Some families listened to the radio, while others made their own music with drums and instruments. One old man in a white headdress was playing a reed that sounded like a bagpipe. Alaa pointed out that he was breathing in and out almost simultaneously. His red cheeks bulged as he squeezed out the melody.

At a curve in the road, Alaa leaned over a stone railing. 'I would like to go to New York,' he confided, looking toward the horizon. 'But I've heard it's dangerous there, that everyone has guns. Do you think I would be safe?' I smiled and thought of my grandmother, sitting in her Brooklyn apartment and worrying about the violence in Israel. 'I want to travel,' Alaa told me, 'but I want to come back home. I know Dier Hanna is the best place in the world.' He gave a satisfied sigh, gazing at the village lights that receded into the distance like stars.

We walked on until we came to Motlak's courtyard. Leading me up an outdoor staircase, Alaa suddenly turned, grinning.

'Where you sleep tonight?' he whispered. 'With me? Sleep with me?'

The question was not so surprising this time. I knew how to handle overeager teenage boys. 'No,' I replied firmly. 'I'll sleep alone.'

He threw up his hands as his father had. 'You can sleep in my room alone,' he promised. 'I give you a key to lock the door.'

Inside the family's small apartment, Alaa's mother had left a set of clean nightclothes folded for me. I heard snoring and saw that Motlak had gone to sleep just outside the threshold of Alaa's room, as though he were keeping watch. To reach the bathroom, I had to step over his sleeping body.

When I came back, Alaa's room was dark, but I heard someone call my name. Alaa was sitting on the bed. Reaching out to me, he hissed, 'Kiss me!'

It was all so dramatic that I couldn't keep from laughing. Alaa looked wounded. 'You don't understand me,' he said moodily, handing me the room key. 'I just want to remember you!'

He gazed up at me with unguarded curiosity, like the girls with the colouring book or the boy who had crawled onto my lap. I tried to imagine what he was seeing – a Jewish stranger as exotic to him as Dier Hanna was to me. I dropped a kiss on the top of his head.

'There,' I told him. 'Now you can remember me.' He left the room and I climbed into bed alone.

All night I could hear Motlak snoring and see Alaa tossing in bed through a small window. All night I could feel the presence of the thousands of lights twinkling throughout the Galilee. At four in the morning I heard a rooster, then a voice over a loudspeaker singing the Muslim call to worship. It wasn't worry that kept me awake. The day's fear and magic combined to form a state of heightened awareness. Lines by the poet Rumi tumbled through my mind:

The breeze at dawn has secrets to tell you.
Don't go back to sleep.

You must ask for what you really want.
Don't go back to sleep.
People are going back and forth across the doorsill where
the two worlds touch.
The door is round and open.
Don't go back to sleep.

The next evening, I sat with Allon and Nimrah at the top of the hill. P'ninah had been furious with Allon for leaving me in the Arab village. She'd ordered him to drive back for me, but he had waited stubbornly for my return. Now he listened, fascinated, to my Dier Hanna stories.

The sky was clear that night. The Sea of Galilee shimmered in one direction, and in the other we could just make out the Mediterranean. Deeper in the hills, a curved red parachute sailed above it all.

'This is a good place to paraglide,' Allon commented. 'It gets dangerous further east. Too close to Syria. You could drift down and find yourself on the wrong side of the line.' Nimrah settled back against his shoulder.

'So how do you like our Israel?' she asked me.

'It feels like home,' I admitted, lying back in the grass.

'Then why don't you move here?' Allon said, grinning. 'There's something special, you have to admit it. It's not like this in America.' The three of us looked up in silence. The moon was rising and distant melodies began to climb the hillside. I lay beside my friends, intrigued by what I knew and they didn't. I knew where the music was coming from. I'd seen the night sky from inside an Arab village, something I wondered if they would ever do.

Allon saw my face. 'She's hearing the music,' he teased. 'Just watch, she's going to follow it down there again.'

I laughed. For all my spirit of adventure, I was happy to be back with my Jewish friends. It would be good to sleep soundly, and the next morning, to head back to a familiar city. I was looking forward to sharing the previous day's adventures with my cousins, and later with friends back home, savouring the whole thing as a far-off, fantastical memory.

But that night, after Allon and Nimrah were asleep, I found myself lying awake again. I came outside in my pyjama pants and tank top and sat cross-legged, my palms resting on the ground. I sat alone and I listened.

The Way I Look

ANTHONY SATTIN

Travelling is not simply part of Anthony Sattin's life, but is also the core of his work as a writer, critic and broadcaster, on both radio and TV. He is the author of many books, including the highly acclaimed *The Pharaoh's Shadow* and most recently *The Gates of Africa*, the previously untold story of the world's first geographical society and the race for Timbuktu. The British *Daily Mail* has called him 'a cross between Indiana Jones and a John Buchan hero'. He is based in London, where he is a regular contributor to the *Sunday Times*, and travels around the world, but his heart flits between the Middle East and Africa.

SOME FACES encourage familiarity. Often, on first sight, you believe you have seen them before, only you can't quite place where it was you last saw them. Other times, you are left with the feeling you know where they have come from. I have one of those faces, and when I travel, this has consequences. In France, I am asked if I am Spanish, in Spain Italian, in Syria Lebanese, and when I checked in at Heathrow for a flight to Tel Aviv, the young Israeli security people were particularly thorough in their examination of my bag and papers. 'Do you have friends or family in Israel? Do you know any Arabs?'

Like most people with knowledge of the Middle East and an awareness of the complexities of the Israeli-Palestinian conflict, I was both heartened and depressed in 1987 by the outbreak of the first *intifada*. It was certainly an escalation in the standoff between the two sides, and for that it was to be deplored. But it was just possible that it might also provide the sort of leverage needed to persuade the Israeli leadership to discuss their differences with their neighbours. The main reason for this lay in the violent heart of the conflict: Israelis were using sophisticated battlefield weapons against Palestinian children and teenagers armed with stones and burning tyres. The imagery looked bad for Israel – it was as though the Palestinians had taken note of one of Jewish history's favourite stories: for stones against tanks, read David against Goliath.

I had already spent several years in the Middle East, and much of that time in Israel and the Palestinian territories. I did not know everything about the conflict, but I knew enough to be convinced that the two sides had more in common than the differences that divided them. As a writer I wanted to commit that thought to paper, so I approached one of Britian's bigger-circulation broadsheet newspapers and suggested writing a feature about how ordinary people on both sides felt on the first anniversary of the *intifada*. The anniversary fell at the beginning of December, which provided me with the idea for the route my journey should take. I was going to travel from Nazareth to

185

Bethlehem, making a peaceful pilgrimage through both Israeli and Palestinian towns, and the paper would run the story on Christmas Eve. And for a reason that seemed to make sense at the time – it would bring me closer to people – I decided to walk.

I arrived in Israel a few days before the anniversary and headed for Jerusalem, not to the holy sites but to the American Colony Hotel in the Arab part of the city. The hotel was a meeting place for foreign correspondents covering the conflict, from whom I was hoping to hear the latest news from the territories. The following evening in the hotel's cellar, with slick, sure-handed Palestinian Ibrahim keeping our glasses filled, I heard several foreign correspondents describe how the Israelis were cracking down, closing entire towns, circling them with armoured vehicles, bulldozing houses, rounding up suspects. Shootings, beatings, dispossessions. Palestinians, on the other hand, were attacking Israeli troops all along my route. The West Bank towns of Jenin, Nablus and Ramallah were in a state of crisis, with groups of young Arabs throwing stones and burning tyres in protest at Israeli occupation. 'We are so proud,' said one elderly Palestinian who had lived through decades of Israeli occupation, bitter but inactive. 'At least they don't have guns,' was the journalists' mantra. There was no denying the seriousness of the situation, brought home to me when one of the correspondents took me to visit a Palestinian hospital where we saw the latest victims of Israeli gunfire. After we had left the grim-faced doctors and distraught families, he warned me to keep out of the way of Israeli soldiers. 'They won't thank you for being there and will happily "mistake" you for a Palestinian,' he said.

The nuns in the convent just up the road from Nazareth's Church of the Nativity took a different line: they seemed entirely unsurprised by my intentions. True, the situation was as serious as any of them had known it, and the oldest of them had been in the Holy Land for more than forty years. But what could be more natural than to make a pilgrimage from Nazareth to Bethlehem? People had been doing so for many centuries. To prove their point, they led me down a staircase beneath their church and showed me an excavated Crusader chapel and, beneath that, a settlement from the time of Jesus. Walking down through the millennia helped calm my anxieties and put the current madness into perspective. I began to look forward to the journey again.

On the morning I set out, the nuns offered their prayers for my safe arrival and wished me Godspeed. It was a glorious day. The bright winter sun shone on God's own country and Israel's rich northern plains glowed brilliant green in the slanting light. I followed the boundary fences of several collective farms before turning up towards the rockier Palestinian lands. There was little traffic and I walked with a spring in my step. Then I reached a barricade of wire and spikes, blocking the road, overlooked by an impromptu army post. This was the unofficial border between Israel and the lands the Israelis had captured in the 1967 war. Against a soundtrack of beeping military communication handsets, an Israel Defense Forces (IDF) soldier raised his machine gun and asked for my papers.

'You cannot come through here,' he barked.

'Why not?'

'The area is sealed off.' When he saw my British passport, he softened his tone and explained that there was trouble ahead. 'It is not safe for you. Are you Jewish?' he asked. 'You know you look like one. It will not be safe for you if the Palestinians find you. And what do you think you are doing by walking? You must go back. If you want to go to Bethlehem, take the Egged bus and change in Jerusalem.'

Half a kilometre back up the road, out of sight of the soldiers, I flagged down a battered nine-seat Mercedes limousine that served as Palestinian public transport, a communal taxi. '*Es-salaam aleikum*', peace be with you. The car was going as far as Jenin, the first Palestinian town along the road. Space was made for me on the least-favoured back bench; three of us were crammed in there, squeezed at the hip, knees near our chins, heads against the roof. I passed a small amount forward as my fare and then the radio was turned up. They were listening to reports of fighting across the Palestinian territories with a grim air of determination about them. The radio was turned off when we reached the checkpoint at which I had been turned away, the car slowed and I hunkered down in the seat. But the soldiers didn't even look: they appeared to be holding random inspections and we were waved on without stopping.

After the anxiety of the checkpoint had passed, my neighbours allowed their curiosity to get the better of them and asked where I was going, where I had come from and why. They didn't have to ask how I spoke Arabic – they could tell from my accent that I had spent time in Egypt. I explained that I had wanted to walk to Bethlehem, but that Israeli soldiers had turned me back. Each answer was repeated slowly and clearly to an old man who sat next to the driver. He was buttoned up in an old tweed coat, had a keffiyeh wrapped around his head and a paper bag of roasted sunflower seeds in his hand. With each response, he nodded and then spat sunflower husks onto the floor. Eventually, like everyone else except for the driver, he turned to look at this Englishman who had spent time in Egypt, spoke some Arabic and was trying to walk to Bethlehem – 'Beit Lehem', as he called it – if only the Israelis (they called them 'the Jews') would let him.

If only the obstacles were so simple.

I knew I would have to change cars at Jenin. Depots for communal taxis tend to be on the outskirts of towns and I expected it to be a matter of stepping out of one car and into another. No need to expose myself in town. But Jenin turned out to have two stations: one for taxis to Nazareth and the north, the other for Jerusalem, Bethlehem and the south. I was going to have to walk between the two, through the centre of town.

The driver explained how to get to the other station. Head down the main street, left at the first junction, carry on straight – and so on. There was an acrid smell in the air, but otherwise the northern station seemed normal. As I came closer to the centre, the smell gave way to smoke, the street emptied. Lines of shops had their shutters down, all daubed with pro-*intifada* and pro-Arafat slogans. The surface of the street was covered with pebbles, stones, rocks and boulders. Along it stormed an IDF jeep, lights flashing, its windows protected, a soldier pointing his machine gun along the road. I heard their communications radio fade into the distance and assumed I was out of trouble. Around the next corner, however, I walked straight into a group of eight or ten young Palestinians. We all stopped. There was a face-off.

Unlike the men in the taxi, the teenagers did not ask where I had come from, nor were they interested in where I was going or what I wanted. But they did care who I was. The one in front said loudly, simply, with hatred, 'He is a Jew,' by which he meant I was an Israeli. This condemnation carried serious penalties, instant punishment: a couple of his friends stooped for stones.

'*La-aa*,' I insisted. No, I am not.

My denial had no effect: they had been badly treated and they wanted revenge. The chaos around us, the shattered buildings, far-off sirens, broken stone and glass and the bitter stench in the air and also, I suppose, the fact that it was so close to the anniversary all helped to raise tension. My knees began to shake, my heart raced. It was clear to me that I was going to get hurt. More than that I refused to consider. Nevertheless, I knew then the full sensation – the taste, smell, touch, sound and sight – of fear.

'He's not a Jew, he's a Christian.' The speaker was the old man from the taxi, hands in his tweed coat. 'He is on his way to Nazareth.' He made no gesture to me, didn't take his hands out of his pockets, hardly even slowed his step or raised his voice. A throwaway comment. He could so easily have kept quiet and continued on his way, but he had chosen to speak and in doing so had saved me from being stoned. He carried on towards his part of town, I hurried on to the Jerusalem station, the boys went elsewhere looking for ways to vent their anger. I never even learned the name of this man whose kindness had saved me.

A couple of days later, I walked out of Jerusalem on the Bethlehem road. The previous night in the American Colony Hotel

I had heard stories of people being shot and stoned. In Bethlehem there had been riots; a tight curfew was imposed. I was ready for the IDF barrier at the entrance to town and insisted on my right to enter. Like the soldier a couple of days earlier, the teenager at the barrier warned me to watch out – I looked like a Jew.

There were other reasons for staying out of Bethlehem that December day. The shops were shuttered, Manger Square was dominated by an Israeli police post, there was desperation in the souk and priests in the Church of the Nativity complained that Israeli soldiers had desecrated the holy place. That night, I was the only guest at the Palace, a far-from-palatial hotel beside Manger Square, but I was treated as part of the family. The manager shared his food with me and introduced me to his friends and colleagues as the Englishman who had come from Nazareth. When he went out, later that night, I asked if I could go with him. 'No, Anthony,' he explained, 'it is not safe out. There is a curfew. There will be trouble. And the Israelis' – that word, 'Jews', again – 'will think you are one of us.'

Late that night I lay awake on an old metal-framed bed, shivering in the cold, listening to the sound of screaming, of gunfire, sirens and smashing glass. The following day I took a Palestinian *service* taxi and headed home.

The newspaper carried my story that Christmas Eve and I hope it encouraged a few people in Britain to muse on the similarities between Israelis and Palestinians. The two sides continued to fight until peace was brokered; a new era seemed about to dawn. Catching the optimism of the moment, I flew to the Red Sea and wrote a story about the proximity – both in distance and in culture – of Arabs and Jews. To illustrate the point, I ate the same beans for breakfast in Egypt, lunch in Israel and dinner in Jordan.

All that now seems a long time ago. Gunmen and suicide bombers have replaced the stone-throwers of the first *intifada*. The Israeli Defense Forces now uses tanks, helicopter gunships and F16s against Palestinian towns, and the two sides seem further apart that ever. At times, peace seems an impossibility. Then I remember the anxious Israeli soldier who warned me to be careful because I looked like him and the Palestinians might stone me. I remember the Palestinians in Bethlehem who told me not to go outside because the Israelis would be sure to mistake me for an Arab and shoot me. I remember the old man in Jenin who saved me from being stoned. I like to imagine a moment in which I am able to bring them all together, introduce them to each other and explain the part they have played in my story. Above all, I like to imagine a time when they see beyond the anger, frustration and hatred and recognise the familiarity of the people next door.

Finding Shelter

Nicholas Crane

Nicholas Crane is the author of *Clear Waters Rising, Two Degrees West, The Great Bicycle Adventure* and *A Mountain Walk Across Europe*. His latest book is *Mercator: The Man Who Mapped the Planet* – the bestselling biography of the world's greatest mapmaker.

THIS STORY – this true story – concerns reciprocal kindnesses in a country which has come to symbolise humanity's trials. The events took place fifteen years ago in the Hindu Kush mountains of Afghanistan, and were recorded in twelve notebooks whose pages were filled by torch light each evening. It's a story which begins and ends in a stone shelter . . .

We had been in the shelter for half an hour or so when Qudous raised himself into the wind, his shoulders hunched against the cold. As he walked away, his footsteps left a broken line in the snow. He must have realised that we were watching his receding outline because he turned after a few minutes and waved.

The five of us crouched on our haunches, backs to the wall. The shelter was barely waist high. It was set in the centre of a valley, and it caught the force of the wind which gusted down from the pass we had crossed that afternoon. We were tired, hungry, cold and anxious. With scraps of kindling, the two horsemen lit a fire.

Six weeks earlier, we had tramped up this same valley, fit and expectant. The sun had been intense and the grass as soft as velvet. In a mujahideen tent camp hidden behind the crags above the shelter we now inhabited, we had dozed through the afternoon heat on blankets laid beside an American ground-to-air missile. It was the last summer of the Soviet occupation of Afghanistan and the Cold War was stuttering to a close. For ten years the Western press had reported on the ragtag bands of horsemen who had held at bay one of the world's two superpowers. Now that superpower was withdrawing from its ill-advised Afghan adventure. In London, the newspapers had been full of conflicting 'pull-out stories': 'Soviet soldiers begin to leave Afghanistan' crowed the front page of the *Daily Telegraph*; 'A dignified retreat' announced the *Independent*; 'Russians set for a scorched earth escape' warned the *Sunday Times* correspondent from Kandahar.

It didn't take a geopolitical genius to grasp that the Soviet departure would not herald the end of Afghanistan's woes. The invaders were leaving a communist regime besieged by several fractious, heavily armed warlords, and they were leaving a homeless population of around eight million. Since 1985, the British private voluntary organisation Afghanaid had been sending small humanitarian teams across the border to Afghanistan with food, medicine and other essential supplies. Through an odd series of circumstances I had become one half of a two-man team charged with evaluating the need for emergency aid among the scattered refugees of the Hindu Kush. Specifically, we were to travel to the Panjshir Valley to monitor the efficacy of the previous year's aid distribution, and to undertake a war-damage survey which would help decision-makers in New York and London to allocate funds for reconstruction.

The job description suited me well: they needed a geographer who could ride a horse and climb mountains. My companion, Julian, was an old Afghan hand, the veteran of several aid trips and the survivor of a close encounter with Soviet gunships. The previous year, Julian's team had been beaten up and robbed. In separate Hindu Kush incidents that year, a British television cameraman had been murdered at his bivouac, an entire tranche of aid money had been stolen from a Swedish mission, and a UN convoy had been hijacked. So, discretion was part of the package.

In a remote valley in the western Himalaya I had sloughed my Western trekking kit and pulled on a baggy *shalwar kameez* and flat cap – the Afghan *pakul.* An unconvincing beard completed the charade. Resting on a pickup bonnet I'd written my will, then pushed it into a brown envelope along with my passport and wallet. Once we had crossed the border into Afghanistan, there would be no contact with the outside world. The pile of dusty clothes on the ground belonged to another person, a privileged tourist who had always seen the wilderness as a natural wonder, who had viewed ethnic diversity as a source of curiosity and comparison. The impending journey would change all that – the mountains ahead of us were a defence system scattered with antipersonnel mines and divided by exposed passes.

For six days we walked and rode on horseback through the mountains, sleeping under the stars or crammed like so many maize cobs into fetid *chaikhanas* (tea houses) whose locations were known to our two guides, Qudous and Jabbar. Both men had grown up in the Panjshir. I'd read of this valley as a teenager, when I'd found in my grandparents' bookshelves a copy of Eric Newby's Afghan adventure *A Short Walk in the Hindu Kush*. Visiting in the 1950s, Newby had depicted the Panjshir as a lost paradise, a place where children played hide and seek in 'enchanted forests' of wheat and corn; a place of heaped apricots and of mulberries which dropped earthward 'in an endless shower'. Newby wrote of poplar groves and dappled willows; of families happily threshing; of women in pretty blues and reds and of little boys in embroidered hats. It was, Newby recalled, 'like some golden age of human happiness, attained sometimes by children, more rarely by grown-ups, and it communicated its magic in some degree to all of us.'

On 7 September we walked the horses down from the final pass into the Panjshir village of Dashte Rewat. Among the bomb craters and roofless houses there was little movement. Every wall was pitted with bullets and shrapnel. Where trees had once shaded the way, there were now rows of stumps. Mutilated beyond belief, Newby's paradise had been pulverised by eight Soviet offensives in ten years. Of the Panjshir's pre-war population of 29,000 families, only about 7000 remained, hidden away in the more remote reaches of the valley.

We slept on the roof of the Mujahideen Hotel and in the morning hitched a ride down the valley in a captured Soviet jeep. Whole villages had been reduced to rubble and dust. Burned-out tanks, armoured personnel carriers and trucks were scattered around the valley floor. A bridge we crossed had been fashioned from a salvaged lorry chassis and sections of tank track.

For the next three weeks we walked and rode up and down the Panjshir, interviewing village headmen and conducting our census of destruction. In village after village we listened to tales of savagery and fortitude. The Soviets had systematically mined the irrigation channels or blasted them from the cliffs. There was a desperate shortage of seed, of timber, of oxen, of water. One man we met had run from his house as the bombs fell. When he looked back, a vast crater occupied the site of his house. Another villager had rebuilt his house four times. And, he said, he would rebuild it next time it was flattened. Miras Abdullah, a mullah from the village of Rockha, had once had ten in his family. One son had been killed and another had lost a leg when he stood on a mine. Before the war, his livestock had included two cows and an ox, ten sheep, one donkey and six goats. 'Now I have no animals,' he told us, 'and I am living under canvas.' His story was typical. Our notebooks filled with lists of loss. And occasional humour: 'Before the war,' said Mohammed Rasi, 'I had nine in my family and I had one horse, one donkey, twenty goats, ten sheep and three cows. Now, my house is completely destroyed and the only animals I have left are one horse and one donkey. My main problem is that I need a Mercedes-Benz.'

We worked hard, pushing the survey close to the Soviet front line and riding far into side valleys. The travelling had a harmonious equivalence: as a traveller, I felt that I was paying my dues, giving as much as I was taking. The surprise lunch of spring onions and chapatis with the headman of a shattered village could be enjoyed with unequivocal rapture; we had earned that meal in sweat and dysentery. But the guilt was always there, the guilt of the privileged voyeur observing misery: I could leave the Hindu Kush for a home in London; the refugees of the Panjshir could choose between battlefield dust or camps in Pakistan.

The survey was completed by the end of September. Work done, it remained for us to extract ourselves from the Hindu Kush with our notebooks before the onset of winter. In leaving the Panjshir, we would become recipients rather than donors of goodwill. Our maps were inadequate to get ourselves out without help, and we had insufficient food and no tents. We would be dependent upon many random kindnesses, and upon our two guides – and friends – Qudous and Jabbar.

The plan had been to return to the outside world by way of a long detour through the northern valleys of the Hindu Kush. We'd begin by crossing the Parendeh Pass to Andarab, where there were rumours of fighting between the *mujahideen* and government forces. London wanted to know whether Andarab was calm enough to receive aid. From Andarab, we would have to cross five more passes before we could leave the country. The journey out would take fourteen days of riding, walking and climbing. There was a chill in the air. Winter had come early. With a brittle excitement, we took to the trail.

Our flight from the Hindu Kush began ominously. Coming down into Andarab's valley we passed the corpse of a villager who had just been shot. And at dusk, as we crouched over the BBC World Service news, a man on the other side of our window fired his Kalashnikov towards neighbouring houses. The cold evening recoiled to sporadic explosions and shots. By morning, one of our horses was missing. Andarab was not 'calm'. We left early.

A couple of days later we crossed the Suchi Pass and arrived for the night at a small hamlet. In a room floored with straw, the eight of us shared a large bowl of rice and then a volcano of mashed bread surrounded by a moat of ghee. By morning, snow was falling.

The horses hated the snow, and the next pass was steep. Cold and tired, we plodded mechanically up the mountainside on a thin, muddy trail through bleak mists. As the trail climbed higher, the wind blew harder, plastering our worn cotton combat jackets with snow and coating beards in tendrils of ice. That night we crammed into a tiny hut and ate cold rice in the dark. The talk was of passes and, in particular, of the Kafir Kotal, the greatest obstacle on our escape route through the Hindu Kush. If it proved to be iced, the horsemen would not be able to cross.

Our little troupe withdrew into individual cocoons. After weeks of concentrating on completing our survey, I was now obsessively concerned with my own skin. Life had been reduced to two self-ish issues: would the passes get blocked with snow before we could reach them, and where would the next food come from? There was little to be done about the former anxiety, except to encourage the general notion that we should walk and ride for as many hours of each day as was physically possible. The food issue depended upon the ability of Qudous and Jabbar to procure rations at the sporadic *chaikhanas* and hamlets along the trail. There were occasional, mouthwatering surprises. In a bazaar, Qudous managed to find a huge bowl of soup into which chunks of bread were mashed. The eight of us scooped hungrily at the sludge with our fingers. At another trail halt, eggs appeared. In a village set on a green lawn below a bright wall of icy peaks, one man welcomed us with tea and small, hard doughnuts. I greeted each of these unexpected treats with pathetic outpourings of gratitude.

Every day the snow line crept lower down the mountain flanks. As we rode and walked eastward, we began to gather rumours of trouble on the passes ahead. An Afghan struggled into a *chaikhana* with news that people were turning back from the Wishti Pass. And then Qudous heard on the 'talkie-walkie' (the trail's word-of-mouth message relay) of a great storm that had killed five men and over a hundred horses on the Kafir Kotal.

At the foot of the Wishti, we unexpectedly came to a *chaikhana,* a shadowy, warm cave of a place. Cross-legged we sat on a goat-coloured carpet and sipped tea from china bowls. Jabbar handed out dried mulberries to chew on the climb. 'For the mountain,' he smiled, pressing his forehead.

Devilled with stomach cramps, I suffered on the Wishti and got left far behind the horses. We came down the pass to another *chaikhana* and I slumped against the wall of a long, thin room while Qudous boiled rice in the cold. The 'talkie-walkie' had revised its death toll on the Kafir Kotal to 230 horses and mules. The only alternative to the Kafir Kotal was a longer, lower detour through a valley whose trails were still mined.

It took us two more days to reach the foot of the Kafir Kotal.

By a frozen stream in a lightless defile, the *mujahideen* had erected a pair of tents. The tents were packed with horsemen, refugees and fighters. This was the pass which would divide those who would winter in Afghanistan from those who would winter in Pakistan. Two of our horsemen decided not to risk the pass. We dumped clothing and our medical kit to lighten our packs.

For breakfast somebody shared a few slices of old bread and part of a tin of Pakistani cheese. Then we stepped into the snow.

The approach to the pass was far from straightforward. We had to cross a minefield and then, to avoid more mines, negotiate an awkward traverse across the bald face of a cliff. At a crashed Russian helicopter we paused for a rest, and then began the final climb through the snowclouds.

Late in the afternoon, we emerged into a high, desolate valley. Ahead of us rose the snow-covered head wall of the valley and at its top, the notch which marked the crest of the Kafir Kotal. Zigzags of men and animals were struggling up a polished groove of ice and snow that had been worn into the head wall. Beside the zigzags, a single chute fell from top to bottom, and down this chute tumbled crates of ammunition, rocket-propelled grenades and sacks of grain – all manner of burden released from the top of the pass by an incoming convoy confronted by an impossible descent.

Clawing up the snow beside the zigzags, I was nearly bowled down the head wall by a cartwheeling mule. Scrabbling horses were being anchored by men with ropes. When I fell myself, sliding and spinning downward, I grabbed at a passing rock jutting from the snow, only to find that it was the frozen head of a horse.

In the chaos of that pass I lost the others and it was nearly dark when I lurched into the *chaikhana* on the far side of the Kafir Kotal. Qudous was already there, and he handed me a pint of tea and a bowl of rice. Later, Jabbar and Julian staggered into the *chaikhana*. Jabbar's feet were a mess. Qudous insisted that we press on. Now down to four, he led the way, down, down, down. Long after dark, we stumbled into a large, spotlessly carpeted tent. Another temporary *chaikhana*, this one run by Nuristanis.

Somehow, they knocked up a meal of boiled rice and tender chunks of meat. By morning our two remaining horsemen were with us.

The next day there was another pass. The last climb, it marked the border between Afghanistan and Pakistan. In blinding sunlight, we walked through deep pillows of new snow. Behind us, the entire horizon was jewelled with diamonded peaks.

Qudous led the way down, into a long, cold valley. And it was here, in the floor of that valley, that we found the low stone shelter. The final leg of the journey required a *mujahideen* guide to lead us through the cliffs to the valley far below. 'You wait here,' said Qudous. 'I will go ahead and arrange for the guide.'

So we waited at the shelter. Qudous had promised to find a guide. And he would.

On the Trail of the Caspian Tiger

TIM CAHILL

Tim Cahill is the author of innumerable magazine articles and eight books, the most recent of which is *Hold the Enlightenment: More Travel, Less Bliss*. He is the co-author of the IMAX film *Everest* and two other Academy Award-nominated motion pictures. He lives in Montana with his partner Linnea Larson.

SAIM GÜCLÜ WAS TO be our minder. We imagined that he'd report back to the government of Turkey about our movements and our motives. We'd contracted for our own driver, but the various government agencies had become intransigent: Saim would be our man, we'd travel with him, in his car, with a driver supplied by him, and the privilege would cost us petrol plus US$300 a day if we took pictures in any national park. People were shooting one another in the national parks we needed to visit and the roads to them were lined with military checkpoints. We weren't going to get through any of them without our official minder.

So we waited for Saim at a hotel on Lake Van, in southeastern Turkey. And while we waited, I reviewed my notes, concentrating on the comments of a number of foreign correspondents for major news organisations.

'Ha ha ha,' is what they had said to us in Istanbul, or words to that effect.

'You will,' they had assured us, 'never get to the southeast area of the country.' This was in early December of 2000, and there were the remnants of a revolution going on there at the time: the Marxist PKK (Kurdish Workers Party) was engaged in intermittent skirmishes with the Turkish military. As a result, Turkish officials were not allowing journalists into the area. A BBC crew had been expelled only a week ago, as had an American journalist who'd ventured a bridge too far.

In the following days, as we sat in offices in Istanbul and Ankara seeking travel permits from numerous agencies, I got the impression that while Turkish officials expressed deep concern for our safety in the area, this was not a paramount issue. I believed that these fine administrators did not want to read another journalistic effort which made the Kurds out to be a swell ethnic minority oppressed by the evil Turks. This article had been written so many times that it even had a name: the Cuddly Kurd Terrible Turk story.

But we – myself, writer Thomas Goltz and photographer Rob Howard – were not going into this sensitive area to write about the ongoing insurrection. Oh no. We were going in under what many of our colleagues thought was the most laughable cover story ever devised. 'You think anyone will seriously believe that you are looking for a tiger?' they asked us.

'They will believe us,' I said, 'because we are pure of heart.'

'Then you buy the next round and we'll tell you why it's not going to happen.'

The borders with Iran and Iraq, in the mountainous south-eastern part of the country where we wanted to go, were particularly hot at this time. There had, for instance, just been a shoot-out in the town of Semdinli. Unfortunately, our research suggested that this was the area where we were most likely to find traces of the Caspian tiger, a huge beast, almost three metres from nose to tail, and the second biggest tiger on earth, after the Siberian species. The Caspian tiger wasn't just elusive; it was con-sidered to be extinct. The last one had supposedly been shot in the southern Turkish town of Uludere in 1970. Now Turkish con-servation groups were hearing scattered reports of tiger sightings on the border of Iraq, where Turks and revolutionary Kurds had been shooting at one another for sixteen years. We thought we'd go take a look. What could possibly go wrong?

Saim Güclü, as it turned out. Our instructions, from the offices of the military and the media, said that Saim would meet us in the town of Van, at the finest of the local hotels, on the shores of the lake that some people say was the original Garden of Eden. The lobby was deserted, but Saim arrived right on time, just about noon. He was a big, well-fed man in his early sixties, dressed for a tiger hunt in a sports jacket and jumper, and he walked with that delicate grace often seen in full-bellied men. He smiled incessantly, in a way that was so sincerely merry I felt subtly menaced. The smile lived under a full and extravagant white moustache.

Saim said that he was the Chief Engineer of the National Forest in this area of eastern Anatolia. He did not fit my image of a ranger. This was definitely not a guy who could keep up with the rest of us on foot. I wondered if we could ditch him, or if that would lead to our arrest and expulsion.

It was too late to start for tiger country: the sun would set by four on this December day. We were in the lower latitudes, yes, but Turkey doesn't divide itself into time zones, reasoning, I think, that such separations might give citizens secessionist ideas. Consequently, if we left immediately, we would be passing through military checkpoints in the dark – which is sometimes a fatal notion and certainly not a good idea under any circumstance.

We decided to spend the afternoon visiting an island in Lake Van where there were the remains of a fourth-century Armenian church. The lake was blue under a crisp sky and snow glittered on the mountains above. If Adam and Eve had spent the entire year here naked, they were a couple of tough monkeys. The temperature hovered right around freezing.

The church was adorned with various friezes: Saint George and the dragon, Cain and Abel, and Moses, among others. At the base of the Byzantine dome, there were depictions of animals. The tiger was the most prominent of these creatures. Rob shot some photos.

'Ha,' Saim said, in his merry way, 'now you pay three hundred dollars.' Was he serious?

'Yeah, ha ha,' I said.

Somehow the idea of the tiger was receding rapidly in my mental rear-view mirror. Perhaps I could salvage something of the story by doing a quick piece about the Van cat. This is a creature that looks like an ordinary fuzzy white Persian cat except that one eye is blue and the other is green. There was a hideous poured concrete sculpture of just such a cat with her kitten on the highway entering Van. The coloured eyes glittered oddly out of the grey concrete. Rob shot a few pictures and Saim said, 'Three hundred dollars.'

'Right.' But now the sun was going down and we needed to get across town quick, to the university, where there was a Van cat genetic conservation program going on in a building called the

Kedi Evi, literally the 'Cat House'. It was Ramadan and pious Muslims had been fasting and refraining from drinking water all day. When the sun set, the feast was on. We bashed through traffic in Saim's forestry truck, racing Ramadan to the Cat House.

It was a two-storey building on the shores of Lake Van, all done up rather elegantly in polished hardwoods. A young man named Mehmet Atarbayir met us at the door, which was festooned with signs reading: 'We are animals. We are an essential part of nature, please don't kill us. In other countries, our relatives are happy but in the heaven that is Turkey it is wrong to make us animals live in hell.'

Mehmet Atarbayir was in a kind of hell at that moment. It was his job to show us about and his dinner was only ten minutes away. He escorted us into the central courtyard, which was fenced. There were a few kittens playing among the wild flowers in the grass growing under a giant skylight. Down the long hallway there was a series of doors with large windows in them. Behind the windows there were furnished rooms – radiators and old couches and bookshelves and dressers. Stretched out and lolling about on all this furniture were any number of odd-eyed Van cats. They looked like feline versions of Salvador Dali's melted clocks.

I interviewed Mehmet, who was so hungry his brain couldn't get out of low gear. Were the cats intelligent? Yes. How did he know? He just did. What did they do? Couldn't I see what they did? What happened when Mehmet went into the rooms? The cats sat on his lap and purred.

Mehmet, probably contemplating dinner, was hustling us out the front door just as the sun set and I was reduced to asking the most moronic of journalistic questions. 'What,' I said, 'is the funniest thing that ever happens in the Van Cat House?'

The young man drew himself up to his full height and said, 'I would never say anything to demean my charges, the cats.' He said this with such obvious sincerity and respect that I squelched a huge burst of laughter bubbling up in my chest. I glanced at Saim. He had turned his back and was faking a series of coughs.

Mehmet felt the necessity to restate his answer: 'Nothing funny ever happens in the Van Cat House,' he said angrily.

And we all burst into laughter. Saim fell into my arms and we hooted helplessly for some time, two hefty guys holding one another and shaking. From a distance, we might have looked like men mourning a fallen comrade.

The cats in the Cat House broke our mutual distrust. Over the next few weeks we became colleagues, then friends. Saim was, in fact, a ranger, but the wildlife section of the forestry department had only been established in 1994. The Kurdish insurrection had started eight years before. No one from forestry had been in the southeast area to inventory animals. 'This is exciting for me,' Saim said. 'But I am ashamed to say that this is work we should have done years ago.'

Saim was able to talk us through several of the checkpoints that had stymied our journalistic colleagues. We were deeper into Turkey than any foreigners had been in some time. In between searches at the checkpoints, Saim and I talked tigers.

We were meeting men in towns like Semdinli who swore they'd seen tracks. Saim had them describe these tracks and draw them in a notebook. There were lynx and a kind of Anatolian panther in the mountains and Saim didn't want to make any mistakes. It was a sad irony that the animals – the tigers and goats and bears – were coming back in the areas where the fighting was the most fierce, where the trails were mined and it was risking your life to be seen in the forest with a rifle. No one had hunted the area in sixteen years. And now the animals were coming back. Even, it appeared, the tiger.

In Semdinli, a Turkish Army colonel listened to Saim and apologised that we couldn't walk the forest, searching for scat. However, he did allow us to go on a military manoeuvre which involved armoured personnel carriers and several dozen armed Kurdish village guards, allied with the Turks. In the towns along the border with Iraq, we met with folks who knew the mountains. There was some controversy, but enough people had had encounters with something very like a tiger that I was becoming convinced it still existed. Saim thought so, too. 'I'm about 50 per cent certain they are still up there in the mountains,' he said.

In Uludere, where the last known Caspian tiger had been shot, the subgovernor, whom Saim later called a 'son of a goat', threatened to confiscate our film. It was best to simply flee. Saim herded us into the forestry truck and we went speeding off down the highway, past a small picturesque village of houses built from river rock. The town was deserted and only parts of the stone walls still stood. The whole place had been demolished by field artillery. Saim stared at the devastation, in a place where Turkey could have been heaven. His face coloured and a vein stood out on his forehead. He said, 'Whoever did this to these people – the military or the revolutionaries – may Allah strike them blind.' Which was my feeling on the matter as well.

We fled south and west, along the border with Iraq, and parted in the city of Sirnac, which was protected by a checkpoint manned by obstinate soldiers who decided the Americans should be imprisoned until officers had a chance to interrogate us. This did not sound like any fun at all and Saim worked his magic, talking to more and more senior officers until he found one who was intrigued by the idea that an extinct tiger still existed in the mountains surrounding us. 'Go,' the officer said. 'Don't let anyone see you in Sirnac. I do this for the tiger.'

We parted in that city, Saim and I. The forestry truck was parked in front of a sweet shop where Thomas, Rob and I found a driver willing to take us to the Iraq border. We transferred our gear, then I hugged Saim and he kissed my cheeks, thrice, in the Turkish manner. He would not take the money that we owed him.

'The tiger,' he said, 'does not belong to Turkey or America or Iraq. We do this for the world.'

'Yeah, but Saim,' I said, 'we owe you a couple of thousand dollars.'

He shook his head and smiled his merry smile. 'The tiger,' he said, 'is without price.'

A crowd was beginning to gather about us as we argued. Bad news. On this trip, in this area of Turkey, every time we had attracted a crowd – in Uludere, in Semdinli – the police had come quickly. Within minutes. And we definitely weren't supposed to be in Sirnac. We had maybe two minutes until the cops came and put us in a cell to await interrogation.

Saim used our trepidation. 'Go,' he said, in his kind way. And that is what we did, feeling that we owed more than money to the Turkish ranger.

The Road to Kampala

STANLEY STEWART

Stanley Stewart has enjoyed the kindness of strangers on countless journeys in over fifty countries. His travel stories, which have appeared in the *Sunday Times*, the *Daily Telegraph* and *Condé Nast Traveller*, have won numerous awards. He is the author of *Old Serpent Nile*, *Frontiers of Heaven* and, most recently, *In the Empire of Genghis Khan*, an account of a 1600-kilometre ride by horse across Mongolia. He has twice been the winner of the prestigious Thomas Cook Travel Book of the Year Award. He was born in Ireland, grew up in Canada and lives in England.

THE SOLDIERS SAID they were going to Kampala the next day. They said they would take me for fifty dollars. Behind dark glasses, their eyes were difficult to read.

Luke, who ran the guesthouse at the top of the town, whistled through his teeth. 'Travelling with soldiers,' he said. 'It's like dancing with the devil.'

But I had already decided to take the chance. Stories about the dangers of the road to Kampala were the gossip of the bars and street corners of Gulu: stories about roadblocks and rival militias and casual violence. Buses no longer went to Kampala, and few private vehicles would risk the journey. Perhaps an army truck was the only way to get through. I paid the soldiers ten dollars 'for petrol' as a down payment, and they wandered away up the street between the buildings pockmarked with bullet holes and the rusting skeletons of old cars abandoned by people who had fled the country.

Luke was right of course. In Uganda in those days soldiers had the worst kind of reputation. Ill-paid, ill-disciplined and deranged by the proximity of death, they preyed ruthlessly upon the civilian population. I knew it was foolish to deal with them, but Gulu offered no other options.

The soldiers arrived the next morning in an army truck and were already drunk, presumably having spent my petrol money to fuel themselves. I paid the rest of the 'fare' and climbed into the back with my bag.

A nightmare ride began. The driver treated the truck like a fairground ride. Twisting the steering wheel, he swung the big lorry back and forth on the narrow road. Laughing in the cab, the soldiers drank beer and threw the empty bottles out the windows at passers-by.

When the driver tired of his game, he found a new one. To the hilarity of his companions, he began to aim the truck at the people along the roadside – women carrying water and wood to their huts, children herding goats and a few cows. Alerted by the roar of the engine, the people leapt to safety across a ditch into the long grass. There were a few near misses. Once we hit a goat which had panicked and hesitated. There was a squeal and then the sickening thud beneath the wheels. Behind us, enveloped in clouds of dust, a boy gazed down at his family's source of milk, reduced to roadkill.

When it emerged, after an hour on the road, that the soldiers were not going to Kampala at all, it seemed a blessing. They threw me off the lorry at Kamudini, a dusty junction, before taking the road east to Lira where fighting had been reported. Waving my money at me through the open window, they drove away in high spirits.

After they were gone, I stood in the middle of the empty highway and listened to the drone of insects, a single note piercing the noon silence. Gulu was now eighty kilometres behind me, too far to return on foot in daylight. Kampala was still well over 150 kilometres to the south. I was alone on a road that no one trusted any more, in a country that had disintegrated. On one thing, everyone agreed. No one who valued their life should be on this road at night.

I picked up my bag and walked south, towards the Nile.

In the old days everyone spoke warmly of Uganda. They called it the Pearl of Africa, and enthused about the beauty of its landscapes and the charm of its people. 'Uganda is a fairy tale,' wrote Winston Churchill in 1908. 'You climb up a railway instead of a beanstalk, and at the end there is a wonderful new world.'

Its descent into chaos after independence was the usual story of post-colonial tensions, tribalism, corruption and economic degeneration. By the early 1970s Idi Amin had seized power, and the country entered a period of dark infamy. By the mid-1980s, when I arrived in Uganda, Milton Obote was back in power but the horrors that had been unleashed in the Amin period continued unabated. Peace would eventually come to Uganda in 1986, a peace on which it has built a future, once again, as one of the bright hopes of Africa. But in those years, the country was still established in the world consciousness as a metaphor for horror.

At the Karuma Falls, the Nile tumbles over low shelves of rock. I stood on the bridge and gazed down into the turbulent waters. I had followed this river almost five thousand kilometres from its mouth at Rashid, and I thought longingly now of the Egyptian Nile, the wide reliable river, the giver of life, which the Pharaohs had elevated to the status of a god. In Uganda the Nile was a different character. Here the riotous vegetation flourished without any help from the river or any threat from encroaching desert. In these landscapes of rain, the Nile was humbled. It seemed to steal through the country almost unnoticed, a silent witness to the horrors. The Karuma Falls was one of the places where the bodies were buried. Army lorries arrived at night to dump corpses into the dark waters. In those years it was said that the only creatures to flourish in Uganda were the Nile crocodiles, the antediluvian emblems of this river.

As I leant on the rail two soldiers emerged from a shack on the bank below and began to make their way up to the bridge. Their broken boots flapped as they walked. I groaned inwardly, and steeled myself for the usual importunities – the demands for cigarettes, for my watch, for money.

But the two soldiers who joined me on the bridge seemed to belong to another world, to the older courteous instincts of this country, rather than the trauma of recent years. They spoke in quiet, shy voices. They called me brother. They inquired if they 'might know my good name', a polite way of asking to see my passport. Having done their duty, they invited me to their shack for tea. They produced dry biscuits from their meagre stores and a supply of mangoes. We sat together on the banks of the Nile as contentedly as picnickers on the South Downs.

I did not ask them how they had come to be here. I did not want to break the spell by touching upon the troubles of the country. But somehow I imagined they had been posted on this bridge years ago, perhaps in those promising days of early independence, when the country was at peace. Somehow the ensuing civil war had passed them by, and they had remained here at their post waiting for further orders from headquarters, orders which never came, as headquarters changed hands from one band of irregulars to another.

Their little hut on the river bank seemed inviolate. It had acquired a domestic air. Laundry was spread across the thatch, and a woman, presumably a wife, was sifting corn in the beaten yard at the rear. In these dangerous times, these men seemed to have found a separate peace. I was not sure if this was founded in innocence or wisdom.

They were dismayed to learn that I was travelling to Kampala. There was little traffic on the road, they said, and no one would stop for strangers, not even for a *muzungu*, a foreigner. There had been too much trouble. No one wished to be delayed. Above all no one wanted to be on the road to Kampala after dark when the roadblocks appeared. Too many people had disappeared.

But their dismay quickly turned to action. We will find a lift for you, they said. Don't worry. We will stop any vehicle that comes this way. We will get you a lift.

It was the hitchhiker's dream – the assistance of armed soldiers to dissuade passing vehicles from passing. Up on the bridge we waited, kicking a deflated football back and forth.

For a full hour, nothing appeared. Then a small pick-up truck came down the hill. The soldiers waved it to a stop and chatted to the driver. He was a local man, only going a mile up the road. The next vehicle was an army lorry. My friends waved me off the bridge into the undergrowth from where we watched it careening past. I wondered if this had been their strategy for survival here at the bridge – judicious retreat.

In the early afternoon a third vehicle appeared – a new Peugeot. It slowed at the first sign of my soldiers, and drew cautiously to a halt in the middle of the bridge. The driver, who lowered his window nervously, seemed relieved by the relatively innocent request to give a lift to a harmless-looking foreigner.

The soldiers shook my hand, and patted me on the back.

'Goodbye, Mr Stanley,' they said. 'God speed.'

I climbed into the back of the car, and waved to them through the rear window. In their broken boots and patched uniforms, my rescuers stood in the middle of the empty road, their hands aloft. In a country that had lost its senses, I felt almost tearful as I watched them diminishing behind us – their simple goodness reduced to a dot in the distance. Then the road dipped and they disappeared.

Once we were out of sight of the soldiers the driver of the car visibly relaxed. He introduced himself as Paul. He spoke English with an American accent.

'I went to college in the States,' he explained. 'Did aerospace engineering at UCLA.'

He was a large man in his thirties with fleshy shoulders and a developing paunch. He wore a pair of pressed trousers and a blue polo shirt. He was a Ugandan but his years abroad had given him the appearance and manner of an expatriate. The car contained the trappings of a cosmopolitan world: an attaché case, a hanging suit carrier, a cooler, glossy business magazines, and fishing rods and fancy tackle – the equipment of sport not survival. On the road to Kampala, Paul was as much a curiosity as I was.

Beside him on the front seat sat a second man. He was small and bony, and his clothes had the exhausted look of hand-me-downs. Paul did not bother to introduce him, as if he did not belong to our world, or we to his. As the drive progressed it became apparent that the man worked for Paul, as a sort of Man Friday. He sat very upright, his hands in his lap, his legs straight, with a self-contained African stillness.

Paul sprawled behind the wheel. He explained that he lived in Kampala and had been in Gulu overnight to see about some business opportunities. I thought of the smashed-up town and wondered what opportunities there could possibly be.

'Reconstruction,' Paul said, as if reading my mind.

The road topped a hill and sunlight glinted on the asphalt far ahead. Here and there ragged banana groves spoke of habitation, somewhere out of sight, away from the road, hidden by the blank face of the bush. Away to the west the mountains of Zaire, as it was still called then, rose from a bed of blue clouds.

'They say this road isn't safe,' Paul spoke over his shoulder. 'They claim it is so dangerous. But I haven't seen any problems. There is a lot of exaggeration in this country. Things get out of proportion. Someone encounters a problem once, and stories begin to spread like a virus. In Africa, there are always stories.'

These reassurances were as much for himself as they were for me. He had come home from America to set up business in Uganda, to bring up a young family, and he needed to believe that things were better than people claimed.

'There is so much rubbish written about this country,' Paul went on. 'Sure there are a few problems here and there, but hell, you can get mugged in New York. There are criminals everywhere.'

Man Friday was silent, watching the road ahead.

The sky darkened and a chill wind blew in through the windows. A storm descended suddenly, the rain sweeping over the road in long gusts, dancing on the tarmac. Far ahead the road shone like a river.

In a moment the sky lifted again and the sun revealed a new world of dense colour. The air had been washed clear and the tarmac, still gleaming from the rain, was barred with sun and shadow from the eucalyptus trees along the edge of the road.

In this post-deluge landscape the car began to misfire. It coughed and spluttered until finally the car stalled on the brow of a hill. We got out and examined the engine. Eventually we got it to start, and drove on. But after a few miles, the engine coughed and stalled again. We went on like this for some time, stalling, starting, then stalling again.

'It is the fuel,' Paul said. 'I should know never to buy fuel out of jerry cans. There is always dirt in it.'

The car became progressively worse. Paul grew agitated, as Man Friday patiently blew on the fuel line and pumped the carburettor.

We were still a long way from Kampala and night was coming on. It had grown cold and the road was empty. Standing on the roadside with the bonnet up, the landscape appeared vast and alien and comfortless. There seemed to be nowhere to turn for help.

We were rescued by two young Swedes, travelling in the other direction. They worked for the Red Cross. Digging a tool kit out of the back seat of their car, they took the carburettor apart and cleaned it. Then they drained the tank and gave us a can of fresh petrol.

'How far are you going?' they asked.

'Kampala,' I said.

They were wiping their hands on rags. 'This road isn't safe at night,' they said. 'We wouldn't advise going to Kampala.'

'I am with this man,' I said. 'He lives in Kampala.'

'Be careful,' they said. 'Four Europeans were shot on this road earlier this year.'

We drove on. Even Paul had fallen silent now. The problems with the fuel had delayed us considerably. We were still over an hour from Kampala, and the sun was setting across darkening bush. It caught momentarily in the tousled heads of distant trees, then slipped behind the horizon. The dark came with equatorial suddenness.

We were entering the Luwero Triangle, one of those tragic places whose name will always be tainted by the horrors which occurred there. Obote's army had been let loose on the area to rout the militias of rival tribes and the villagers who supported them. The young men had been rounded up and taken to prisons in Kampala where they were routinely tortured and killed. The rest of the population was terrorised. Abduction, rape, torture and murder were commonplace. Every week in the shells of burnt-out villages, in roadside ditches, in forest clearings, mutilated bodies were found. Their crime was that they were members of the wrong tribe.

As we drove we saw nothing out of the dark windows but our own imperfect reflections. The wheels battered in and out of potholes, as the night's chill crept into the car.

In the headlights a roadblock appeared – a long pole between two barrels. Paul drew up before the pole, switched off the engine and the headlights, then turned on the interior lights. We sat in the car like illuminated exhibits, unable to see anything in the darkness around us. This was the form. They wanted to see you, without being seen themselves.

But we could feel them around the car, something restive and menacing. Slowly shapes emerged out of the darkness, about a dozen men cradling guns, soldiers of one militia or another. One of the men came to Paul's window, his rifle scraping carelessly along the door panel.

He leaned into the car. He was chewing something. His lips were wet. He looked at us one by one. The sour smell of his sweat filled the car. Finally his rheumy eyes came back to Paul.

'You have something for me?' he said at last.

Paul dug in his breast pocket and handed him some money. The soldier looked at the bills, assessing the amount, then straightened up slowly and motioned with his rifle for the pole to be lifted. The car started and we drove on.

The empty road floated in the headlights, untethered to the dark country, a strip of illuminated asphalt suspended in a void. After fifteen kilometres or so, another roadblock appeared. We drew up before the pole and extinguished our headlights again. As we sat waiting in the car with the interior lights on, we could hear someone groaning in the darkness, the pitiful whimpering noise of a man in pain.

Suddenly a voice barked at us. 'Get out of the car.'

We climbed out.

'Go to the front,' the voice shouted.

We walked forward and stood in the road in front of the car. A figure leaned through the car window and turned on the headlights. Blinded in the glare, we waited for long tense minutes as the invisible soldiers assessed us. When the voice came again it made us all jump.

'Who are you? What are your names?'

A soldier had appeared on the periphery of the light. Behind him we could see the ghostly figures of other soldiers. All of them had their rifles trained on us.

Paul gave his name. Then Man Friday gave his. I was about to give mine when the soldier lowered his rifle and stepped forward. He greeted Paul in a quiet voice and they shook hands. They stood talking for a moment in the language of their tribe. Their names had revealed Paul and Man Friday to be Acholi. At this roadblock, it was the right tribe. After a brief exchange we got back into the car. From somewhere close by, I could hear the man, someone from the wrong tribe, still whimpering in the darkness.

Beyond the next hill the lights of Kampala appeared. We drove through its devastated streets to the suburb where Paul lived on one of the hills above the town. He had offered to put me up for the night. It might be dangerous, he confessed, to look for a hotel at this hour.

In the morning, from my window, I could see Lake Victoria, the source of the Nile, as blue and indifferent as heaven.

At a Crossroads

LAURIE McANDISH KING

Laurie McAndish King has studied medicinal plants in the rainforests of Brazil and Argentina, chased lemurs through the mountains of Madagascar, fought off leeches in tropical Queensland and studied with an urban shaman in San Francisco. When she isn't working for a living, she is trapping and banding raptors in northern California. This is her first book publication.

I DIDN'T KNOW whether I was being kidnapped or rescued – that was what made my one big decision so difficult. That, and the fact that I was young and foolish and more than a little anxious about being stranded in the North African desert.

It all began quite innocently. Our bus had deposited Alan, my affable travelling companion, and myself at the door of a small, clean hotel in a dusty Tunisian village. The buildings were two storeys high at most, covered with plaster and whitewashed against the powdery red dust that enveloped the town and seemed to stretch forever. In the desperate heat of late afternoon, the place appeared to be completely deserted. Not a single shop was open and the dirt streets were empty: no vehicles, no pedestrians, not even a stray dog.

Inside, the 1940s-era hotel was as empty as the street. There were no brochures advertising nearby attractions (I suspected there were no nearby attractions); there was no 'We accept VISA, MasterCard and American Express' sign. That was okay; I had travellers cheques. There was no bouquet of silk flowers, no table, no couch on which weary travellers could rest. A lone, white straight-backed chair stood sentry on the floor of exquisitely patterned blue and red ceramic tiles. The reception desk held a silver tray filled with Christmas mints – the round green kind with a red Christmas tree in the middle – like my grandmother used to put out every year. It was August, and they looked old.

I had only just met Alan, a wandering college student like myself, that morning. But I quickly decided he'd be great to travel with: he seemed friendly, calm and reasonable – not the type to freak out if a bus schedule changed or a train was delayed. Plus he spoke a little French, which I did not. Alan had a quick, cryptic conversation with the hotel clerk, and then translated for me. The clerk had suggested that he hitch a ride to the local bar/restaurant – ten kilometres out of town – for a beer and a bite to eat. It didn't occur to either of us that a woman shouldn't also venture out, and I was eager to see some sights, meet the locals and have dinner. Of course I went along.

In retrospect, I realise I should have known better. We were in Tunisia, a country where women stay indoors and cover up like caterpillars in cocoons. The guidebooks had warned me to cover my shoulders and legs, and I felt quite modest and accommodating in a button-up shirt and baggy jeans.

When we arrived, I found that the place was more bar than restaurant, and that I was the only female present. Even the waiters were all men. But these details didn't seem important. After all, I had dressed conservatively, and decided to take the precaution – again, recommended by my guidebook – of avoiding direct eye contact with men. What could possibly go wrong?

Since I spoke neither French nor Arabic – and was assiduously avoiding eye contact – it was quite impossible for me to converse with anyone but Alan, who was busy putting his first-year college language skills to dubious use. I was bored. This was a plain-as-bread sort of establishment; there was no big screen TV soccer game, no video arcade, not even a friendly game of cards or a good-natured bar fight for me to watch. Just a lot of dark men in white robes, sitting in mismatched wooden chairs, speaking softly in a language I could not understand, and drinking tiny cups of strong coffee. The bitter, familiar aroma was a meagre comfort.

Then the music began. It sounded off key and was startlingly loud and foreign – a little frightening, even. Next the belly dancers appeared: twelve gorgeous women, one after another, with long, dark hair, burnished skin, flowing diaphanous skirts in brilliant vermillion and aqua and emerald, gold necklaces, belts, bracelets and anklets. Gold everywhere: tangled cords jangling against long brown necks; fine, weightless strands decorating the swirling fabrics; heavy gold chains slapping in a satisfying way against ample abdominal flesh. They were a remarkable contrast to the stark room and simple furnishings, and I began to realise that things in Tunisia were not entirely as they first appeared.

The music quickened, and the dancers floated across the bar – which had somehow been converted into a stage – and around the room, weaving in and out among tables, lingering occasionally for a long glance at a pleased patron. Soon they were at our table, looking not at Alan but at me, urging me, with their universal body language, to join them.

Did I dare? My stomach clenched momentarily. I knew my dancing would be clumsy and ugly next to theirs; my short-cropped hair and lack of make-up unattractively boyish; my clothing shapeless and without style or significant colour. I wore no jewellery – as the guidebook suggested – just my glasses, which were not particularly flattering.

Of course I was relatively unattractive and clumsy in this foreign environment, I thought, but there was no need to be priggish as well. And the women were by now insistent, actually taking me by both hands and pulling me up to dance with them. Flushed with embarrassment, I did my best to follow their swaying hips and graceful arm movements as we made our way around the room once again. Even with the aid of two beers, I was not foolish enough to attempt to duplicate their astonishing abdominal undulations.

As soon as I thought these exotic, insistent beauties would allow it, I broke the line and resumed my place – plain, awkward, very white and completely out of my element – next to Alan. Thereafter, it was excruciatingly embarrassing for me to watch the dancers, and Alan agreed to accompany me back to the hotel. He, too, had had enough excitement for the evening and was ready to retire, so he asked the bartender to call us a cab. A fellow bar patron overheard the conversation and was kind enough to offer us a lift. The man wore Western-style clothing, understood Alan's French and seemed safe enough; we felt fortunate to have arranged the ride in spite of our limited linguistic abilities and the fact that the night was still young.

But that's when the evening turned ugly. Two well-dressed, middle-aged men left the bar immediately after we did. We saw them get into a black Mercedes, and we watched in the rear-view mirror as they trailed us, just our car and theirs, bumping along a sandy road in the empty desert. There were no buildings, street-lights or pedestrians, and we saw no other vehicles.

I looked out the window, enjoying the vast, black night sky and trying to ignore my growing sense of anxiety. When we came to an unmarked Y intersection, our driver, in a bizarrely ineffective attempt at deception, headed steadily towards the road on the right, then veered off at the last second to take the road on the left. Neither Alan nor I could remember which direction we'd come from hours earlier, when it was still light out and we were not under the spell of Tunisian music and belly dancers and beer. The strange feigning and last-second careening alarmed us both.

And it got worse. Immediately after the incident at the intersection, the men in the car behind us revved the engine, chased us down and ran us off the road and into a ditch. They got out of their car and stood near our window, shouting and gesticulating wildly. My hands went icy in the warm night air. Despite, or perhaps because of, an imposing language barrier, we had the impression that the men who ran our car off the road were attempting to rescue us.

But what, exactly, were they rescuing us from? Was our driver a sociopathic kidnapper bent on selling us into slavery? A rapist? A murderer? And why were our 'rescuers' so insistent? Was it out of the goodness of their hearts, or did they, too, have some sinister motive? We had to make a choice. One car would probably take us safely to our hotel; the other might lead to a terrifying fate. But we had no idea which was which.

In this moment of crisis, we clenched hands and Alan looked at me – somewhat desperately, I thought – for a decision. I tried to assess his strength and wondered whether he was a good fighter. (Probably not – he was a Yale man.) My stomach churned, but I forced myself to concentrate. We had only two options: we could remain in the long black limo, hope it could be extricated from the ditch, and hope our volunteer driver really was the kind and innocuous man he had appeared to be. Or we could bolt from the car, scramble out of the ditch, and as quickly as possible put our rescuers and their car between ourselves and the man who had so generously offered us a ride. The two men were still shouting and began to pound and slap our driver's window. Even so, Alan leaned towards staying. After all, he reasoned, it was only one man and there were two of us. Surely we could overpower him and escape if it proved necessary.

I wanted to bolt. Even though there were two men in the 'rescue' car, as opposed to only one in our vehicle, I had become certain, in some wholly subjective way, that our man was crazy, and I'd heard that crazy people could be quite strong. Plus, our apparent rescuers – the men who had just run us off the road – warned Alan that we were with '*un homme mauvais*!' A wicked man. But the deciding factor was that these two men had actually gone to the trouble of following us out of the bar, chasing us down, running our car off the road and into a dusty ditch, and were now expending a great deal of energy trying to convince us of something.

Surely that constellation of actions bespoke a serious purpose, such as rescuing two foolish young travellers from a lifetime of misery in the North African desert. The two men must be rescuers; kidnappers were not likely to go to so much trouble, or to risk scratching or even denting their shiny late-model Mercedes in the process.

Alan was no help; I had to make a decision myself, and quickly. But what about the downside? In the middle of all the commotion – and with Alan sitting next to me looking more than a little uncertain – I realised that we had not yet fully considered the potential outcome of an incorrect choice. If we chose to stay, and it was the wrong choice, the man would undoubtedly drive us to some sort of central kidnapping headquarters – probably an impenetrable, fortress-like stone building with dark, echoing corridors, or perhaps a sweltering, waterless hovel cleverly hidden in remote, sand-swept dunes. In that case, he would have a knife, or a gun, or evil partners – or perhaps all of the above – and the fact that the two of us probably could have overpowered him would be moot. We would be goners.

On the other hand, if we bolted, and that was the wrong choice, we would be double-goners because the two men could also turn out to be kidnappers or murderers who could easily overpower us. Downsides being equally awful, we decided to go with our gut. Or guts. The problem was that Alan's gut said stay and mine said bolt.

Fortunately, it didn't occur to either of us to split up. Eventually I was able to convince Alan to bolt, which we did with great vigor, clawing through weeds and rocks and dust, out of the ditch, onto the road and into the cool, black car waiting in the darkness.

But even then we couldn't relax. As we rode off into the night – this time with two men in the front seat – my stomach was still churning; we had no way of knowing whether we had made the right decision. What if these men were evil? Perhaps we had been unwittingly trapped in some web of rival-kidnapping-gang intrigue from which there was no hope of escape. Or perhaps it had begun even earlier, with Alan's fractured French, or with my being the thirteenth dancer – and in pants.

Eventually our two rescuers returned us to the Y intersection, turned onto the right – and correct – road, and delivered us to the hotel without further incident. God forgive us, I'm pretty sure Alan and I were both too dazed to thank them. Well, we thanked them for the ride, but not for saving our lives.

Inside the hotel, my stomach calmed down and my hands returned to their normal temperature. The stress began to drain from my body; at last I could enjoy the luxury of relief. Alan and I stood at the reception desk, looking into each other's eyes. He picked up a Christmas mint from the silver bowl and ate it. I could smell it on his breath. The entrance hall was cool and quiet; no one else was around.

'Well, that was quite an evening,' he finally said.

'Yes, quite an evening,' I agreed.

'Well, goodnight, then.'

'Okay, goodnight.'

I walked upstairs, puked and went to bed.

Adnan's Secret

MAXINE ROSE SCHUR

Maxine Rose Schur is an award-winning travel essayist and children's book author. She teaches travel writing workshops and is a guest speaker at conferences and universities throughout the United States. More information about her can be found at www.maxineroseschur.com.

HIGH IN THE PINE-COVERED mountains of southern Turkey lie the ruins of the only city Alexander the Great could not conquer. Termessos is its name.

In January, when the air is dry and crackling, and the sage bushes – from which the Turks make *ata çay* (healing tea) – have grown scraggly, there are few visitors. This is the time to come to Termessos. And this is when we came.

The first written mention of the city was in 335 BC when Alexander the Great, sweeping across the Pamphylian plains, came up against a people who fought him so furiously that, after burning their olive groves, he moved on.

We hiked up the long dirt path, passing a sprinkling of shepherds' huts. When we arrived at the top, we were surprised by the sight of a magnificent Greek theatre curled into the hillside. Walking about the ruins, we discovered among the weeds the remnants of a gymnasium, an agora and a collection of sarcophagi strewn haphazardly up and down the hills by an earthquake more than two thousand years ago. Beyond the tombs, we came to the rim of the plateau, where we could look out across the winter-coloured valleys below. The cool air carried the smell of bay and mint. Chimney smoke wafted faintly from the shepherd huts. In the silence, broken only by the occasional bleating of a lamb, we felt all the beauty of Termessos was ours to enjoy alone.

'They're Americans! Americans!'

We looked around to find where this voice came from and, turning, saw at some distance two figures sitting on rocks. 'They're Americans. I know it!' Walking closer, we saw a large man in his sixties, well dressed and eating stuffed grape leaves straight out of a can. A tiny camp stove was boiling water for tea, the tin kettle tended by a Turk, also well dressed and smiling.

'I told you I saw Americans!' the large man laughed and, turning to us, asked, 'You are Americans, aren't you?'

This was our introduction to Mr Brand, a wealthy, retired Canadian executive who was now touring the ancient ruins of

Turkey, rolling about the countryside in a Mercedes-Benz belonging to his friend and personal guide, Adnan. Adnan stepped forward to introduce himself. His manner was of the city – refined and confident. He seemed a highly educated man, and later we learned he had worked for the Turkish Intelligence.

It was obvious that Mr Brand was tickled to find fellow North Americans in this isolated place, even if they were scruffy, poor and half his age.

'Which hotel are you in?' he asked us. When we answered that we had travelled from Switzerland, living mostly in our van, he looked at us incredulously and then laughed at the surprise of it.

'Come to my hotel in Korkuteli tonight!' he proclaimed. 'We'll have dinner at seven and you'll be my guests!'

That evening when we entered the hotel's small dining room, we saw that all the tables were empty but ours, which glowed with candlelight. 'We are having an international dinner,' Mr Brand announced as he and Adnan ushered us to the table, delightfully set with little paper Turkish, Canadian and American flags.

Mr Brand ordered grandly. We had seemingly endless platters of appetisers followed by a roast lamb dinner. We talked with Mr Brand of many things that evening: politics and food, jobs and TV shows. We created the immediate heartfelt bond travellers experience when they find themselves with superficial things in common far from home. Adnan told us a little of his work for the Turkish government, but most of all he enjoyed joking with Mr Brand, and waggishly dubbed him 'Alexander'. 'You conquered another archaeological site today, Alexander,' he teased. 'You met very little resistance. Very good.'

We swapped endless anecdotes and laughed uproariously at everything and then, just like that, Mr Brand closed his eyes, his head dropped to his chest, and he was asleep. His slumber, however, was not sound, for at intervals he mumbled plaintively, 'Darling . . . darling.'

At these mutterings, Adnan would look at us in mock puzzlement and wickedly ask, 'Excuse me sir, excuse me madam, but did either of you call me "darling"?' The *raki* we were drinking made this repeated joke seem very funny, and with Mr Brand asleep, the three of us continued our conversation in high spirits deep into the evening.

Outside our dining room, stars slowly emerged while, to the regular measure of Mr Brand's snoring, we sipped *raki*.

I thought then how good it was to be in Turkey. We had been warned many times of the dangers of travelling in this country, yet in every town we had experienced only the warmest hospitality.

'I like it here,' I said suddenly. 'People here have been kind to us.'

Adnan put his glass down. 'The people of my country are very good.' His voice had turned solemn and quiet. 'I will tell you how very good my people are.' He began to speak as gently as if he'd just borrowed someone else's voice and had to be especially careful with it. 'I will tell you now what I have never told anyone.' Then, as the candlelight flickered, Adnan tenderly told us his secret.

'You know from our talk this evening that I am a city man. I am no villager, no peasant. My wife too. Let me tell you. Not only does she not cover her hair, it is blond! For many years I worked hard in the service of my government from early in the morning to late at night. On a Saturday night we enjoyed ourselves with friends in Istanbul, but for years I took no vacation. One day, about six years ago, I said to my wife, "Let's get out of the city. Let's visit Izmir province. Let's go to Ayvalik and swim on the beach. We can take a boat to Alibey and the other islands – get away from all thoughts of work." My wife was so happy, she packed right away. The next day we started out. About two hours after we started, we drove through an area you wouldn't know, but the road is very bad, skinny and full of holes. On this road, which passes through a village, I saw coming toward me a cart pulled by a horse. The cart was piled high with potatoes on which sat a whole family. That is the way it is in my country: person or potato, you ride the same.'

'Darling,' Mr Brand softly beseeched. We glanced at him but Adnan did not make his joke.

'The cart came toward me slowly, but I was in a hurry. I had a dream of islands in my head. "Slow down," my wife said. "I am," I answered. "Now don't worry. I will pass him." But I must tell you we have a saying from the Koran, "Haste is the devil," and it is true. For as I passed, I came too close to the cart. Perhaps the horse started, for seconds later I saw in my mirror the cart – fallen over on its side.'

'Was anyone hurt?' I asked.

'Wait, I will tell you. I stopped the car and got out to look. My wife turned around to look, too, and screamed. "Be quiet!" I shouted to her. "Put your scarf on! Cover your head!" Among the potatoes, the family stood, still as statues. As I walked toward them I saw what they were staring at. An old woman lay on the ground, face up. Those who have never seen death might have thought she was asleep, but I knew she was already with Allah.

'I looked up at the faces of her family surrounding me and into the vengeful blue eyes of a tall man,' Adnan paused. 'In your country, everything goes through the courts, but for my people, justice is done by families. Cruel and quick.

'I escaped while they were still stunned. I ran to my car, turned the key and stepped hard on the gas until the family became no more than a tiny reflection in my mirror. Fast as an assassin I drove toward Istanbul, for I had no desire to continue my holiday, and I told my wife this. I drove all the way back home, my wife crying softly beside me. I only stopped once in Manisa to put in gas. They are far from me now, I thought as I drove, and after all, I reasoned with the pride of working for the Turkish Intelligence for eighteen years, they are simple people and would never think to write down my license number.

'The next day I went back to work, my co-workers making a joke of my early return. I made up a crazy reason and laughed with them. Yet that night I could not relax. "I killed an old woman," I said to my wife. But she was now calm and logical. "It was not your fault. They had no right to take up so much of the road. They should pull off the road for cars. You did not mean to hurt anyone. It was an accident. You did not do it on purpose!"

'I knew she was right and after half an hour or so of this kind of talk, we went to bed. But I could not sleep. For the longest time, I just lay in bed, turning from side to side and thinking. Then, quietly, so as not to wake my wife, I got dressed, put on a cap, walked down the stairs and into my car.'

The waiter asked us if we wanted coffees, and after Adnan ordered them, he continued.

'There was little traffic at that time. Only a few trucks heading into Istanbul. I drove continuously, without thinking anything.

'It was morning when I arrived in the village. As soon as I entered the village I knew they were burying the old woman, for I saw groups of people all going to one house carrying food.

'I turned around and drove back out of the village. I parked my car about half a kilometre from it. I pulled the cap tightly on my head, walked back, following the mourners inside. The tiny house was crowded with people sitting on the floor, standing against the wall and in the doorway. "*Basiniz sag olsum*," someone said to me. Let your mind be healthy. "*Basiniz sag olsum*," I returned. In the centre of the room, in her coffin draped with her green embroidered head shawl, lay the old woman. She was wound in her shroud, which was far too long at the feet, and so wrapped around her legs with a rope. About her, the women wailed, but the men stood stone-faced and silent.'

'Weren't you afraid?' we asked.

'I was afraid, and yet there was no other place I wanted to be. The old woman was completely surrounded by mourners. With all those people, it was hot in the room, and from her coffin arose the mingled smells of camphor and rosewater. The *hoca* of the village stood by the coffin, and after a while began to read aloud from the Koran in a sad musical way. Some of the villagers mouthed the words too. I joined in, myself. All the while people kept coming in the door, "*Basiniz sag olsum*!" "*Basiniz sag olsum*!"

'"The cap does not hide you." I heard a whisper in my ear, and turned to find myself looking into a man's deep blue eyes. "I know who you are," he said. "You are the man with the fine car. You parked it behind the mosque, didn't you?"

'I nodded.

"'You are the man from the city. You are license plate 34 LE 047. You are the man that killed my mother."

'Our eyes met. My heart pounded against my chest like a prisoner beating at a door. Words would not come.

'In the next second the man was joined by two others. Now all three of them stared hard at me, and I wondered why I had left my gun in Istanbul.

"'You ran away," the blue-eyed man said.

'My mind raced. "How quickly can I bolt to the door?" I thought, not daring to avert my eyes from his gaze.

"'You ran away," he repeated, "then you came back." He paused. I wanted to say something, perhaps to defend myself, but I said nothing.

"'Only a very brave man would come here. Because you came back, my family forgives you."

'I don't know what I said then. To tell the truth, I probably said nothing, for the words weren't in my mouth anyway but in my heart.

'Suddenly a wail of mourning sounded. The women had begun to weep, and the whole house burst into grief. "Thank you," I said to the blue-eyed man. He said nothing. Our eyes locked for a moment and then he and his brothers turned away. They were going to take their mother out of the house. I watched the little home slowly empty itself, the villagers walking as a group, chanting as they carried the old woman high above their heads. The coffin bobbed up and down – a tiny wooden boat on a gentle sea of mourners. I did not stay to see her buried, but drove away. I arrived back in Istanbul just at the call of the muezzin. It was dusk at that moment, and as I crossed the Galata bridge, the whole city seemed to me sanctified.'

Adnan took a sip of coffee. For a long while he did not speak. Then he said simply, 'That is why I tell you my people are good.'

He paused again as if he were going to say something else, but he didn't. Instead he nudged Mr Brand. 'Alexander, *efendi*, you have more conquests tomorrow. It's time to go to bed, Alexander.'

Mr Brand woke up. We thanked him for the dinner and bid them both goodbye. We climbed into our van in the night-seeming morning, sobered and strengthened by what we had heard. We saw the lights go out in the dining room. The next day we headed to Antalya, to find a hotel or somewhere to stay for a while before continuing east. 'Watch out for the eastern Turks!' we'd been told several times. Yet we would have to cross the path of these people we had been warned about, and briefly, in some fashion, be linked.

As travellers, we were strangers to everyone, and everyone a stranger to us. We had to rely on only the fragile, often surprising connection we knew we could feel with others, and others with us. This is the connection made despite difference, distance and even death. It is the delicate thread of sympathy that stitches humanity together.

Might Be Your Lucky Day

JEFF GREENWALD

During the 1970s Jeff Greenwald hitchhiked back and forth across the USA four times, once along the Canadian route. His books include *Shopping for Buddhas*, *The Size of the World* and, most recently, an anthology entitled *Scratching the Surface: Impressions of Planet Earth, from Hollywood to Shiraz*. Jeff now lives in Oakland, California. Visit his website at www.jeffgreenwald.com.

FERN DUCKED BEHIND the bushes, though there wasn't much in the way of bushes. Sage scrub, mostly, waist high at best. Her modesty was optimistic; no cars had passed for forty-five minutes.

I sat by the road and read *Dune*, listening to her moan. She hadn't been well since we'd left Mexico, abandoning her dying Duster north of Caballo and hitching, with our Camp Trails backpacks, up the Rio Grande towards the Interstate. That was yesterday. With a car of our own, we could reach San Francisco in one long day. But begging rides on this empty road – there was no telling.

You always got a ride, though. Nobody stays in one place forever.

Fern emerged from the bushes staggering, looking dizzy. I closed the book, forgetting to mark my place.

'You all right?'

'I need water.' She opened the pocket of my pack, took out a canteen, and drank too much. It was nearly three in the afternoon. She'd been napping against her backpack, and the impression of a zipper ran, like a fading scar, down her left cheek. Fern was a cream-skinned girl from Minnesota, and the Mexican sun had blistered her nose, cheeks and shoulders. She hadn't tanned anywhere.

Fern stared down the road, looking east. Ponds of mirage mirrored the juncture of asphalt and sky. 'How long have we been here?'

I squinted at the sun. 'Two hours.'

'It's really hot.'

'You can sit under the poncho if you need to. We should probably spread it out, anyway. I folded it wet.'

'Maybe I will.' We sat on our rolled-up sleeping bags. Fern brushed her hair, very slowly. 'I don't feel so good,' she said.

'Listen.'

There was so little noise that we felt the sound as a vibration, transmitted from the road through the bones in our legs. I jumped up, praying for a westbound semi. Trucks had been good to us, the drivers full of stories and happy to buy us lunch – the pretty girl in her peasant blouse, her joker hippie boyfriend.

We waited as the frequency crept up the wavelengths – now a low pulse, the purr of a distant engine, the hum of a car. It was a sedan, long and maroon, with a black vinyl top. I set our packs against each other and we stood in the road, Fern in front, her thumb out, me holding up the ragged square of shirt cardboard with the initials SF crosshatched in red block letters. A big car, with two people in front. It slowed down and rolled to a stop a few metres beyond us. I trotted ahead to the driver's window, which rolled down with a nasal whine.

'Thanks for stopping. Where you headed?'

The driver was in his late twenties, with black hair slicked back above a pirate's stubble, and wearing a loose polo shirt and navy sport jacket. He looked rough and red-eyed, but I liked him on sight. A gold Rolex hung loosely on his right wrist, which rested easily on the steering wheel. A notion came into my head that he'd been the best man at someone's wedding, and had just run off with the maid of honour. He looked me over, grinned and turned to his companion, a bleached blonde who might have been ten years older. 'Where are we headed?' They looked at each other, then exploded into laughter. The woman leaned toward me. 'West,' she whispered, like a spy.

We'd met stranger people. 'Got room for us?'

'You bet.' The driver shut off the car, sorted through the keys and found a round one. 'Throw your stuff in the trunk.' As I moved away: 'Just shove the body to the left!' Hysteria from within. I laughed, too, and jogged over to collect Fern's bag.

It was a smart-looking '74 Monte Carlo, with opera windows and leatherette seats. I opened the trunk and threw in our packs. They seemed small in the cavernous space, framed against the splotched protective carpeting. A spare tyre, a tyre iron and a white golfer's cap were the only other things in there. I hesitated, and arranged our gear to give easier access to the spare.

And then we were moving, the highway going by as the beautiful wind flew in through the front windows and tossed Fern's hair in front of her glasses. Her eyes were already closed.

'You're going to 'Frisco?'

'San Francisco,' I nodded, bristling at the contraction. 'Moved there a year ago. I've never been in this part of the country before.'

'Me neither. Hey, sorry. I'm Tony.' He craned around to pump my hand; his wristwatch rattled.

The woman smiled back at me. 'Sue.'

'Where are you from?'

They answered at the same time. 'Texas,' said Tony, as Sue said, 'Georgia.'

'I'm from Texas, and she's originally from Georgia.'

'Never been to Georgia, either.'

'It's lovely,' said Sue. 'Peaches.'

'How far do you think you can take us?'

They were both silent for a while, exchanging glances, until Tony shrugged and looked back at me. 'Don't know. Our plan was LA. But 'Frisco sounds good, too. Sue?'

'Sure sounds better than LA.'

'See?' Tony pulled down his visor and unclipped a pair of sunglasses. 'Might be your lucky day.'

We passed the first hour talking about the week we'd just spent in Mexico: the tired white buildings and sugared bread and Tweetie Pie piñatas. Fern's old Duster had wheezed through Albuquerque and taken us due south, through Las Cruces and into Ciudad Juárez. It was our first time south of the border. We'd made it as far as Moctezuma, and would have kept on going, but the radiator developed a leak and we had to refill it every hundred kilometres. Rather than give up, we made a wide, dull loop through Galeana and Nuevo Casas Grandes, where a local rancher put us up and fed us cinnamon pancakes. But he kept staring at Fern's breasts, so we snuck out one afternoon and in a single hellish spell drove the Plymouth back over the border, where the valve seals disintegrated. I unscrewed the plates and we abandoned the smoking piece of shit in Truth or Consequences.

Fern slept through all this. But Tony listened like it was the best story he'd ever heard, like I was describing Timbuktu or Fiji instead of the flatlands of Mexico. He drummed on the wheel as the car steered itself, pumping me for details, raising his eyebrows at Sue.

Grants, New Mexico, was the first real town along the Interstate. A quarter century ago, in 1950, a farmer here had found a warm yellow rock on his land. Within months, Grants was as famous for uranium as San Francisco is for sourdough bread. We stopped at a supermarket and collected a loaf of white bread, two pale tomatoes, mustard and packaged cold cuts of turkey and ham. Tony bought a six-pack of Coors.

'What about dessert?' Sue asked.

'One Snickers, a 3 Musketeers, one Baby Ruth and a PayDay,' I said, shaking my bag. 'Take your pick.'

Sue clasped her hands like a little girl, then grabbed Tony's shoulder. 'I like this guy!'

Tony winked at me. 'He's all right.'

There was a Gulf station close to the market. Tony took me aside and asked if I'd help with the gas. 'No problem.' I actually had a Gulf credit card, my one and only, though I hadn't used it since leaving New York eleven months earlier. The attendant filled the tank. I signed the paper slip, jammed the card into my wallet and tossed it into the shallow well on the dashboard.

Just short of Gallup we approached a rest stop. Fern asked Tony to pull over. The minute the car stopped she ran for the toilet, clutching her belly. Tony checked the oil, then wandered off with Sue for a few minutes. In front of the structure with the rest rooms and phones stood a big square kiosk, framing a map of the Four Corners region. When the couple returned we looked it over together.

'So much to see,' I said.

'Like what?' Sue's mouth was moving, adding up miles.

'The Grand Canyon, Bryce, Zion, Monument Valley. I've only seen pictures. When I drove out from the East Coast last May we took Interstate 80, so I never saw the Southwest. Look – there's the Grand Canyon, right there.' The green blotch on the map, girdling the Colorado River, seemed as mysterious as a sixteenth-century map of the New World. 'It's weird to be so close.'

Tony studied the roads and touched his finger to the junction of Highway 64, almost five hundred kilometres away, just beyond Flagstaff. 'If we took this road, we could be there tomorrow.'

'You'd drive to the Grand Canyon?'

'Definitely. I love all that geologic shit.'

Sue glanced at him with a surprised smile. I was slack-jawed, astounded by this potential stroke of good fortune. 'Don't you have to be anywhere?'

'Not really. We're on vacation.'

A number of things that seemed a bit off, a bit wrong, pecked at the burl of my neocortex. 'You guys drove out from Texas, right?'

'Yeah.'

'Well . . . where's all your stuff?'

There was a short silence, during which neither of our bene-factors looked at each other.

'Everything's in LA,' said Tony. 'Sue's father died a couple of weeks ago. We flew out together to pick up his car and figured we'd buy what we needed along the way.'

'Guess you haven't needed much.'

'Not yet. Wait. I bought a toothbrush. And shampoo. And some Trojans.'

'Hey!' Sue punched him.

At that moment Fern emerged from the bathroom. Her fore-head was damp and she looked like she'd been crying. 'I'm sorry,' she said. I brushed her hair away from her eyes and put my arm around her. 'I just feel feverish.'

'Montezuma's revenge,' Tony explained, tapping the map with his knuckles. 'I got it once, in Tijuana. Terrible. You gotta make sure you get plenty to drink. And if you're smart, you'll mix some sugar and salt with your water. Sounds disgusting, but it helps dehydration.'

'Thanks.' Fern sounded unconvinced. 'I better refill the canteen.'

'I'll do it for you,' said Sue. 'Go rest in the car.'

Fern nodded gravely and I helped her into the back seat. I was worried about her, but ignorant about tourista. Whatever she had, I figured, would soon run its course. It certainly didn't seem a good enough reason to give up on the Grand Canyon – or on our new pals. It's funny, the kind of strange, great people you meet when you travel, and how the right combination of personalities can make anything possible. Tony and Sue were strange folk, but I was infatuated with them: spontaneous, easy to laugh, attractive. Despite their lack of jackets, shorts or hiking boots – Tony had black wingtips, while Sue wore oversized pumps – they seemed ready for anything.

'Ever been to the Petrified Forest?' Tony pointed to a brown road sign with white letters, coming up on our right. 'It's eight kilometres ahead.'

Fern and I sat knee to knee in the back seat, making sandwiches on the face of our hitching sign. The radio was tuned to a Flagstaff rock station. Paul Simon faded in and out as we cruised between blasted cliffs and sandstone buttes – 'Still crazy after all these years'. The car smelled ripe.

'Never,' I said, awed by our proximity to the famous park. 'I didn't even know it was near here.'

'We could have a picnic there,' said Sue. 'If Fern's up to it.'

'I can manage. If we park near a rest room.'

We turned south into the park. The scenic drive followed an odd gauntlet of frozen stumps, agate tree rings and Indian pictographs. It was late afternoon and primordial shadows loomed across the road. East of the road, the Painted Desert undulated like an iridescent sheet. After half an hour we reached a little turnoff.

'Blue Mesa,' said Tony. 'Sounds cool.' He steered the Monte Carlo onto the rough loop track. There was no one in sight. 'This is perfect,' he said. I agreed; it felt like the giddy middle of nowhere. We soon reached the trailhead: a parking area with a marker, a bench and chunks of petrified wood scattered around like shavings from some Triassic sawmill. Tony killed the engine, waited for the dust to settle, and rolled down all the windows. He took a huge breath. 'It feels like forever,' he said, 'since I smelled anything this good.'

I got out and walked over to the sign. A scenic walk started here, a one-kilometre round trip. 'I'd like to do it,' I said. 'Shouldn't take more than half an hour.'

'I'll go with you,' Tony said.

'You sure you're okay in those shoes?'

'Fuck it. I'll just wipe 'em off afterward.' He turned to Sue. 'You two staying here?'

'I'm not walking along the edge of a cliff in these. You go right ahead.'

'Have fun,' Fern said.

The Blue Mesa trail loops like a noose. When we reached the farthest point Tony and I stood side-by-side near the drop-off, staring out at the mesa itself: a monolithic pedestal of stone, streaked with gunmetal minerals, rising from the palette of the desert. A steady, warm wind blew up the cliff and across our legs; if we'd had hang-gliders, this would be the place to use them.

'Feels like you could fly,' I said.

Tony stared into the distance. 'What's stopping you?'

'Ha.' I pondered the deeper question. 'My weight, I suppose.'

'Right on.' He pulled a pack of Camels from his coat, offered me a smoke. We lit up together. 'What if I was to help you?'

'What do you mean?'

'I'll do it first.' Tony walked a few steps up to the cliff's sharp edge. A few stones rattled over. He craned his neck to see down – it was ninety metres, at least, to the rocks below – and flicked his cigarette into space. Frantic sparks danced in the updraft. 'Grab the back of my belt.'

'Holy shit. Are you sure?'

'Yeah, do it.'

I did, with both hands. Tony checked the buckle, spread his arms, and leaned forward, over the edge. His eyes were closed. The wind parted his hair, and I could see light brown roots. He wasn't leaning far, but it was enough; he was trusting me with his life.

After about ten seconds he straightened up, whooping and laughing. 'Man! That was amazing!' he said. 'Your turn.'

I took my place on the cliff's edge, Tony behind me. He held my belt with both hands. I leaned forward, eyes open, tilting far enough so that my feet disappeared from my peripheral vision and the land seemed to sail by beneath me, moving at the speed of wind. I howled with elation. This was nuts, we were insane, and I loved it.

Tony tugged me back with sudden force. I felt wildly high and threw my arms around him. But he stiffened, and I backed off. 'Thanks, man.' I shivered once, like a dog. 'Wow. You guys are great. I'm really glad you stopped.'

Tony giggled, an odd sound, and I suddenly wondered how old he was. 'Me, too. Let's check on the girls.'

The Motel 6 in Winslow had one room left, a lower floor corner with peeling walls, a dripping faucet and two double beds with pillows that smelled like stale cigarettes. They wouldn't take my Gulf card. Tony paid cash from a folded sheaf of bills, tucked into the pocket of his shirt. We still had a few leftover sandwiches and two candy bars. Fern didn't eat; Sue bought her a Diet Coke from the machine down the hall.

I carried our packs in from the car and showed Sue and Tony the souvenirs from our trip: some silver earrings, my sketches of a fountain, the water-filled jar of opals that a Mexican farmer had sold me for ten bucks. We let them use our toothpaste and our brush. There was a colour television in the corner, and Tony and I sat on our beds while the girls shared the bathroom. The hit shows that spring were 'All in the Family' and 'M*A*S*H', but this was Wednesday night. We settled for 'Little House on the Prairie'.

'You still up for the drive to the South Rim?'

'Absolutely,' said Tony. 'Maybe even Zion. Long as we can gas it up on your credit card.'

'No problem,' I laughed. 'The bills will go to my folks' house.'

He raised his eyebrows. 'Your family's rich?'

'Naw. But I got the card back in New York and haven't changed the billing address.' I shrugged. 'It won't amount to much.'

We drank tepid beers, discussing the snacks we'd buy for our trip, and whether four people could fit into a two-person tent. Sue came out of the bathroom first, wrapped in a towel; I hit the lights as she climbed into bed with Tony. The water ran for a long time before I heard the toilet flush. The room blinked with light as Fern opened and closed the bathroom door, then slid up shivering against me.

I stirred from deep sleep in the early hours of the morning. The room was black, and the conversation so low it might have been imagined. Fern snored lightly, and I wasn't sure if what I heard was rough breathing, the television next door or the fragments of a whispered nightmare: '. . . one more tank . . . straight through to San Diego . . . south, if we need to whack them . . . just do it fast . . . no, the way I showed you . . . shut up, bell . . . tomorrow, I swear . . . shut up, let me sleep.'

I threw my arm across Fern's back. When I woke again the room was bright and the shower was running. Tony walked in from outside, carrying coffee from the reception lounge. Four black coffees, in Styrofoam cups.

It was less than 120 kilometres to Flagstaff. Fern had used the bathroom at the hotel, but she had to stop again at the rest stop near Two Guns. Tony kept smiling, but I sensed he was restless. Sue hadn't said much at all, and I figured that, like me, she wasn't much of a morning person. Still, Fern's condition wasn't improving, and it was unlikely there would be many facilities on the undivided roads between Flagstaff and Grand Canyon Village.

We sat in the car, listening to the radio. It was already blazing hot and might hit three digits by noon. I was down to shorts, a threadbare Exploratorium T-shirt and rubber flip-flops. The leather of my wallet, on the dashboard facing east, was too hot to touch. After ten minutes Tony opened his door and swung his legs out. His knees popped. 'You sure Fern is all right?'

'She's definitely not all right,' I said.

'She seemed dizzy,' said Sue. 'And she's been in there a long time.'

We sat in silence for a minute. 'I'll see how she's doing,' I said and pushed the heavy door open.

I found Fern in a stall, whimpering with fright. There was blood in the bowl, but it was weeks before her period. 'Something's really wrong,' she said. 'It's not just diarrhoea. I can't keep anything inside.'

I flushed the toilet, led her to the sink and washed her face with a damp towel. She wrapped her arms around my waist. 'I know how much you want to go to the canyon,' she said. 'You can, if you want. But I'm in no shape for a trip. I'll find a ride home from Flagstaff.'

'That's insane. You picked up something in Mexico, that's all.' I closed my eyes, letting the fantasy go. 'We need to take care of you.'

'What should we do?'

'I don't know. Tony and Sue were originally going to Los Angeles. Maybe they'll drive us there and we can get a bus. I bet they'd even take us all the way to San Francisco. They're really great people. And I'll pay the gas.'

A shadow lifted from Fern's eyes, and she radiated relief. It was the first good colour I'd seen on her face in days. 'I'll tell them,' I said. 'Finish washing up.'

I jogged back into the light, which smacked me like a cartoon hammer. And then I got hammered again. The parking lot was empty. There was no Monte Carlo, no sign of Tony or Sue.

I stood stupidly in the sun, looking right and left, looking for our packs under a tree, for a message tacked to the kiosk, for a shady place Tony might have moved the car. There was nothing, anywhere. When Fern came out we stood silently together. Then she put her hands to her mouth and cried. I held her, numb with disbelief. It was nearly twenty minutes before I found a pay phone and called the cops.

We had no money, no ID, nothing but the clothes on our backs. We looked like a couple of lost desert rats, peeling and penniless. A highway patrol car drove us into Flagstaff and dropped us off at an anonymous downtown corner. We didn't even have our canteen. Half an hour later, Fern was on the verge of fainting; somehow, we made our way to the nearest emergency room. She spent the night in intensive care, a drip attached to her arm. One more day on the road could have killed her, the nurse said. While Fern recovered, I scoured the city for a ride west and for any trace of our so-called friends. Both enterprises were futile; this was 1974, and a ragged, unwashed twenty-year-old did not inspire much sympathy among Arizona truckers.

Once Fern was rehydrated and the Flagyl had kicked in, we hitched to the nearest truck stop and made one last effort to find a sympathetic ear. Fern, not surprisingly, was better at this than I was – it was best, in fact, if I stayed out of sight entirely – and her hospital bracelet backed our hard-luck story. In less than twenty-four hours, a tractor-trailer driven by a former boxer named Squidge dropped us off at a ribbon-and-bow outlet near the San Francisco Flower Market.

A week passed. Fern flew back to Minnesota, and life returned to some variation of normal. I didn't tell my parents about the Flagstaff incident. For one thing, I felt like a sucker; and since they disapproved of hitchhiking, this would just give them more ammunition.

It was a beautiful spring. I began a job as a day-camp counsellor with the Jewish community centre on Presidio and California Streets – two easy bus rides from my shared flat in the Sunset. Since I didn't have a car, I didn't bother getting my licence replaced; it was from New York and I needed a new one, anyhow. Most of the possessions I'd had in Tony and Sue's car had been sentimental: my journal, the fire opals, my New York library card, a few pairs of comfortable underpants. Stuff that was either irreplaceable or easy to replace. I didn't even think about the credit card.

One Thursday night, after an awful picnic featuring poison oak and carnivorous wasps, my housemate Kitty rapped irritably on my bedroom door. I squinted at the clock: it was two in the morning. 'It's your father,' she said.

I rolled to my feet and staggered down the hallway. This was weird; it was 5 a.m. in Plainview.

The phone was on the kitchen cutting board. 'Hello?'

'Jeff, is everything okay?'

'Uh . . . yeah. What's going on?'

'Are you sure you're okay?'

'Of course. Why?'

'Okay, explain this.' My father loved to phrase things in terms of riddles. 'At exactly 4.20 a.m., our house was surrounded by squad cars. Six cops pounded on the door. They're looking for you.'

'Me?'

'You. They have a warrant for your arrest. Armed robbery, kidnapping and murder.'

My dad was a prankster, but this was out of his range. I stood breathing quietly, my hand against the ironing board closet, absolutely convinced I was dreaming.

'Are they still there?'

'The police? They're right here. The police, the FBI, God knows who else.'

A voice I didn't recognise came on the line. 'Is this Jeffrey Michael Greenwald?' I realised with a shock our whole conversation had been monitored.

'Yes . . . that's me.'

'This is agent Frank Tennison of the FBI. What's your location, please?'

'I'm at home, in San Francisco.' I paused, then gave him my address. The phone was muffled and I heard the muted sound of discussion.

'Dad, are you still there?'

'I'm right here.'

'Okay. I think I might have an idea what's going on.'

'Maybe you better tell us,' he said. And I did.

There was a tense silence. Tennison spoke next. 'Mr Greenwald? I must advise you not to leave your house. For your own safety. We'll have a car there within fifteen minutes. Do not wait outside.'

Their real names were Sam and Belle. Three weeks ago, they'd stabbed a medic and escaped from the Louisiana Forensic Unit for the Criminally Insane. A day later, an elderly man was found dead in the high grass by a highway outside of Lafayette, a bag of golf clubs lying nearby. They'd taken his car and his cash and fled west, somehow evading the dragnet set up along the main routes leading from Louisiana into Texas, Arkansas and Mississippi.

During the past ten days – after abandoning us at the rest stop near Flagstaff – they'd ducked south to Jerome, and slipped into California. Along the way they had blazed a trail of mayhem, robbing convenience stores and leaving pieces of stolen identification to throw off the police. My library card and driver's licence weren't the only pieces of ID scattered in drugstores and 7-Eleven parking lots. They'd picked up another hitcher in Fresno, taken his wallet and cut his throat.

According to the car's fuel stops – still being charged to my Gulf card – the pair hadn't yet left California. 'They know where you live,' the FBI branch agent informed me, 'and they need a place to hide. They may be crazy enough to come here and create a hostage situation. For that reason, we're offering you protective custody. Alternatively, we can assign an agent to you full time. It's your call.'

It all seemed unreal to me. And though it was easy to imagine how thrilled my campers would be by the sight of a real, live FBI agent, I had a reckless desire to see the fugitives again. What was I thinking? That I'd confront them, of course – and make them pay for their betrayal. Absurd as it was, I thought I deserved an apology.

'No, thanks,' I told the agent. 'I'll look after myself.'

And so I did – with ever-increasing anxiety. Every time a car slowed down behind me, or a Monte Carlo cruised by the community centre's arch, my palms began to sweat. After a week of this, a practical humility replaced my bravado. I swallowed my pride, picked up the phone and called the Golden Gate office of the FBI, ready to send for reinforcements.

My trepidation, as it turned out, was baseless. The killers had been picked up the previous night in Las Vegas. They were now in custody in Nevada.

'Were they still driving the Monte Carlo?' I asked.

'Nope, they'd picked up another car. Another Chevy, in fact.' The agent seemed amused by their brand loyalty.

'Did they find anything in the trunk?'

'They did.'

'And?'

'It was the last guy they'd picked up, cut into six pieces. Forgive me for saying so,' the agent quipped, 'but I'd guess that your backpacks are history.'

Strange, the way a writer's mind works. Nearly thirty years have passed, and I've never recorded that story. I didn't even begin writing travel, really, until four years later, and by then the saga of Tony and Sue had been eclipsed by other encounters, other adventures, in Athens and Cairo, India and Nepal.

Sometimes, when I'm canyoneering in Zion, or hiking the rim of Half Dome, I remember the afternoon Tony and I stood on that Arizona cliff, holding onto each other, our wings spread to catch the thermals. How simple it would have been to be rid of me that moment, by simply letting go of my belt. It could have all ended right there, for Fern as well. God knows, we wouldn't have been the first.

Sue and Tony are gone now, dead or alive, I've no clue where or when. My anger, too, has faded into the past, and I view our encounter in a more generous light. What I focus on now, when I recall those twenty-four hours, is our spontaneous trust – our intoxication with freedom, that shared sense of adventure. For the fugitives, it was a race against time – their calculated risks stretched to breaking by those endless, unnerving pit stops for Fern. How they must have fretted at each rest stop and filling station, their eyes in the rear-view mirrors, weighing the folly of delay.

But they'd loved us, those killers. Far from betraying us, they'd left us with our lives. A spontaneous kindness, freely given, in the idiom of the road.

Ascension in the Moonlight

SIMON WINCHESTER

Simon Winchester, a former foreign correspondent for the *Guardian*, now writes books and divides his time between a farm in the Berkshire Hills of Massachusetts, a flat in Manhattan and a cottage in the Western Isles of Scotland. He is the author of the bestselling *The Surgeon of Crowthorne* (entitled *The Professor and the Madman* in the United States) and *The Map That Changed the World*, as well as numerous other books. His most recent book is *Krakatoa: The Day the World Exploded*.

IT WAS A BLAZING tropical morning in the middle of nowhere. I was on a rusting, salt-stained Russian tramp steamer beating slowly up towards England across the doldrums, and for reasons long forgotten I was in a desperate hurry to get home. We were making no more than eight knots that day, which meant that I'd not see the cranes of any European port for the better part of three more weeks. And out there on those hot high seas – I was on my way back from Antarctica – it was unutterably tedious.

The radar on the bridge showed an Atlantic Ocean surrounding us, entirely empty of everything – except, that is, for the tiny speck of Ascension Island, which lay otherwise invisible, sixty-five kilometres off, on our starboard bow. It was then, in a sudden moment of realisation, that I remembered something. On Ascension Island there was an airfield, and jet planes flew there, to and from London. If I played my cards right, *I could get myself out of here.*

I promptly got on the ship's radio, asking if anyone over on Ascension could possibly hear me. At first, nothing – just the hissing white silence of dead ocean air. But I called and I called, and eventually, quite faintly at first, there came over the ether a British voice. Yes, it said, he was the duty harbour master. What did I need? I told him I wanted to get on the next RAF flight to Britain, and so could I come and land on Ascension and try and wangle my way aboard?

Yes, he replied, after a momentary muffled conversation with someone else, provided that I was fit and able to jump when told to do so – because the Atlantic rollers were making landing at Ascension perilous that day – it should be possible for me to land; and since there was a northbound plane due to arrive in two days, then I might also be able to find a seat and get myself to London in double-quick time. 'Ask your captain to steer towards Ascension,' the man said, 'and when eight hundred metres off, tell him to put you ashore in the whaler. If you're fit,' he said with what sounded like a sinister chuckle, 'you ought to be able to make it.'

Half a day's slow sailing later, and the enormous dark pyramid of Ascension Island rose up directly ahead of us – a mid-ocean volcano, eight hundred metres high, its summit brushed with green foliage and a patch of dark cloud, the slopes and the spreading base iron-grey coloured and seemingly as lifeless as the moon. A few sorry-looking buildings were dotted here and there, and a cluster of radar domes and aerials, and there was a gathering of Nissan huts around the long single runway of the aerodrome.

A grinning Russian sailor who said he had been here once before, and who the captain assured me 'knew the form', lowered me into his whaler, and we motored swiftly off across the chop. We chugged away from the rusty little ship, across to a tiny gap in the Ascension sea wall, a gap in which I could see a narrow set of steps rising up slimily from the waves. Enormous swells and rollers crashed over these steps at regular intervals, completely immersing them, then draining away again in a rush of wild whitewater and fronds of streaming weed. There was a slime-covered rope fasted to a doubtful-looking and very corroded iron stanchion. The Russian told me that all I had to do was to wait for the interval between swells, leap onto the highest step I could manage – the higher I managed, the less slippery the steps, he laughed – and clutch hold of the rope as tightly as I could.

Well, I'm here today, and so the scheme must have worked. All I remember is a welter of confused green water, the precipitous dipping and rising of our whaler's bow, the sudden scream from behind me of 'Now!', my feet and hands scrambling for a hold, the wet length of rope tightening under my weight, the onrushing of the next wave knocking me off balance but the rope holding, holding – and then my furious dash upwards until I was at last onto a dry step. My bag, hurled with great force by the Russian sailor way down below, landed roughly beside me, followed by the yell of *Dosvidanya*! from behind.

And then, quietly, almost like a gentle whisper from my left, came another voice.

'Do let me be the first to welcome you to the British colony of

Ascension Island,' it said. 'My name is Paul Wilson. I am the vicar here. And this is my wife, Angela.'

I turned, and indeed there was, quite unexpectedly, a cleric – a young, fresh-faced clergyman very obviously of the Church of England, dressed in white shorts and a tropical shirt, but with the telltale clerical collar. He was short, fair-haired, very pinkish, precise, rimlessly bespectacled.

The Reverend Paul Wilson, vicar of Saint Mary's, wore an expression that morning of a sincerely concerned kindliness – as did his wife, who looked rather like him, only she was larger and somewhat gawky in a sundress of an old-fashioned chintz print, such that unkind souls might say she looked a little like a small, animated sofa. The pair could not have been anything other than English, two expatriates doing their level best to find suitable employment for themselves during the languid hours of faraway tropical heat. Meeting me, I guessed, was part of what they might have called their *pastoral duties*, ensuring that all was well with their flock on this tiny outpost of what remained of Britain's empire, here in the outermost reaches of an otherwise unpopulated stretch of ocean.

I shook hands, and Paul suggested that I step along towards their house. It was a 500-metre walk to Saint Mary's vicarage, a walk which took us past the old fever hospital and the former lazaretto for African lepers, and past the nineteenth-century barracks that had housed Royal Marines who were stationed on Ascension to make doubly sure that Napoleon would stay put, in his permanent post-Waterloo exile on Saint Helena, a few hundred kilometres to our south.

It was far too hot today, and there was no one about – just a few donkeys, now wild animals that plagued the island just like the feral cats the local people had tried to eliminate some years before. The donkeys chewed the wing mirrors off the local cars, and everybody loathed them.

We walked past the tiny modern bungalow where the administrator worked – no colonial governor was warranted on so small a dependency as this, said Reverend Paul. Then in a low voice he explained that most administrators were men who had 'rather failed to make an impression' during their careers in Britain's diplomatic service.

It was the only unkind thing I ever heard Paul say, though it was evident that neither he nor Angela seemed much to like their posting on the island. Paul had been preaching quite happily, thank you, in a church in Spitalfields in London, when orders had appeared one Monday in the post, suggesting that he might like to take over the Church of Saint Mary's of the High Seas in the Dependency of Ascension. It was a three-year job; there were two hundred people on the island, most of them Saint Helenians working on contract for the airbase, or else secretive expatriates working among the fields of aerials, performing hush-hush work for one of the American spy agencies.

'They call the Saint Helenians "Saints",' said Paul as he opened his garden gate. 'So I imagine they don't really need us, do they?' He chuckled mildly at his own drollery. 'And the Americans don't come to our church. So Angela and I have rather little to do – and frankly we see almost no one. Which is why we were so pleased when they said you were stopping by. You are more than welcome to have lunch, and then please stay with us until the plane comes in tomorrow night.'

Inside there was a salad waiting for me, and a glass of cold beer. 'I expect you'll be very happy with that,' he said, and he winked at his wife conspiratorially, as if a drink at lunchtime was somehow mildly sinful.

And so I stayed in their little rectory for the rest of that day and night, chatting and indulging in what passes for Ascension tourism – which means, primarily, climbing to the top of Green Mountain, then going for a swim in the dewpond at the summit, and signing my name in what must be one of the least-used visitors' books on the planet. From high up on top of the mountain, if the clouds part for long enough, it is possible to see a hundred kilometres in all directions, and the ocean – looking like an unblemished sheet of hammered pewter – stretched empty to every horizon. It was so lonely that I almost shuddered.

During the night the southbound air force jet had come in, on its way down to the Falkland Islands, and so the following morning we had English newspapers and magazines, and I was able to catch up with news and gossip. I had been in the Southern Ocean for the better part of the previous four months, and knew little of the goings-on up north; and now, reading all about it, so much seemed so blessedly irrelevant. Angela was happy, though, and spent her day in the garden contentedly buried in the *Daily Mail* and a copy of the *Tatler*, lobbing pebbles at any donkeys that tried to eat her sandwiches.

Once she looked up from her reverie, and spoke to me. She had a surprise for me later that night, she said with a smile – she would give it to me just before I left. The northbound plane – Paul had managed to get me a seat on it, as had been suggested on the ship's radio – was due in a little before two in the morning. Perhaps, Angela said, if we all took a little siesta – something not too difficult to achieve, in a place that was hot, lonely and exceptionally boring – we could all arrange to go down to the airfield together, and they would see me off. I protested that there was really no need, but they seemed to want to. They apparently had something planned.

I must have slept until ten. It was quite dark when I awoke, and the house was alive with a curiously expectant air. Downstairs I found Paul and Angela dressed in mufti – no dog-collar or chintz, but swimming costumes instead – and packing up a picnic basket. 'Well done, waking now,' said Paul cheerfully. 'We thought we'd go off on an expedition. We'll take you to the only white-sand beach on the island – and when we're there I think we'll see something rather special.

'And by the way – I think Angela said something about a surprise? Well, they came on the jet from England. Fresh strawberries and Devonshire cream! We've not had them for a year! And you've probably gone without such things for ages. So let's take them down to the sea, right away!'

And so, after I had changed into my trunks, we set off in their rickety old Morris Minor – the car that they and their predecessors had all inherited from a vicar back in the sixties – and we swept slowly around the island, past the old colonial buildings and the great airfield and the Nissan huts, until we turned off and bumped down through a rocky defile, and along to a tiny beach, glinting pure white under a fast-rising moon.

As it rose, the soft and sugary sand took on an appearance just like snow – the sea beyond it black, its waves crashing rhythmically on the shore, the rocks behind black also, and in between them this postcard-sized field of the purest white shell powder, illuminated by the immense pale moon, and with a clear sky full of a blizzard of stars.

Angela unpacked the hamper, and she laid out dishes of strawberries and a jug of cream on the blanket, together with three glasses and a bottle of cool white wine. To sharpen our appetite, and to delay the pleasure of the food, we all ran down to the sea and swam for a while, then lay floating beyond the surf, the water warm and velvet soft, and we gazed up at the sky, looking for shooting stars. After fifteen minutes or so Paul looked at his watch. 'Back to the beach!' he cried. 'The show starts soon.'

I had no idea what he meant, but the three of us walked back up to where we had left our things, and sat back and toasted one another with Vouvray and ate the soft fruit and the cool cream, and joked with one another that we were, as Paul and Angela must have known, in some anteroom to heaven. And then Paul cried out.

'Look!' he said, and pointed down to where the waves were crashing onto the beach. 'Quiet!'

I saw it in an instant. It quite startled me. A huge dark shape was lumbering slowly out of the white water, and was heading, inching, up the beach. First one emerged, then another, and another – until there were maybe fifteen of them, moving slowly and almost painfully up the sloping sand, like wounded soldiers of an invasion force. One of them approached within two metres of us – and once so close, I could see exactly what it was.

A green turtle. I had heard about them – Brazilian green turtles, living on Brazil's Atlantic coast and yet choosing, due to some curious quirk of nature, to lay their eggs three thousand kilometres away on this tiny island in the middle of their ocean. And this, precisely, was what each one of these huge, magnificent beasts was doing.

The lady closest to us turned ponderously around so that she was facing the sea, then used her back flippers to scoop out a cavity in the sand. Once it was ninety centimetres or so deep, she quietened herself and concentrated, until, with a strangely, unforgettably intimate sound of chelonian parturition, she expelled a clutch of thirty or forty eggs into the hole. I craned myself up quietly and saw the eggs as they lay, glistening wetly in the moonlight, until their patient mother shovelled sand back on top of them, to protect them and keep them dry.

She seemed utterly exhausted from the effort, quite drained, and for a few understandable moments she rested, until, with what in a man would have been a quite superhuman effort of will, she hoisted herself back down the slope, battered her weary way through the raging surf, and began her long, slow, eggless swim back home again, all the way to Brazil.

For fully an hour the three of us watched, transfixed. Occasionally I could see that Paul was watching me, just to make certain that I was as enraptured as he had been when first he saw the animals. Angela spoke softly as she poured another glass of wine. 'Aren't we just the luckiest people?' she said. 'Isn't this a privilege?'

But that wasn't the half of it. There was more. For at almost the same moment as she asked this rhetorical question, she shivered. I could see her skin was suddenly covered with goose bumps. She drew a beach towel around her shoulders. And I felt it too – a sudden coldness in the air, as though a cloud had materialised from the tropical sky, and blanketed everything in its chill.

But it wasn't a cloud. As I looked up at the moon I could see that the shadow of the earth was now steadily sweeping across its face, and the whole world was darkening again, being turned back to black as this portion of our planet experienced a total lunar eclipse. Suddenly the white sand went dark. I could no longer see Paul or Angela. Only the glow of the distant runway lights spoke of civilisation nearby. Only those lights, and the stars, broke the velvet blackness of the night.

As I looked at the stars I suddenly noticed something else: that in the eastern sky, rising above the dark where the horizon had been, was a bright object that, once I could see it properly, was undeniably *a comet*. A famous, swept-tailed comet, blazing for thousands of miles out in some distant part of the solar system, and now only properly visible because the air was so clear here, and the local world was so inkily black. It was splendid, unbelievably so.

The moon came out of its shadow a few moments later, and the brilliance of the stars faded a little, and the comet became barely visible once again. But just then it had been visible, and I, moreover, had seen it.

And it was in that instant I realised something: that in this astonishing grand conjunction – of new friendship, of tropical warmth, of strawberries and cream and cool white wine, of white sand and sea swimming, and of Brazilian turtles, an eclipse of the moon and the rising of a comet – was perhaps the greatest wealth of experience that any one individual could ever know in one moment. I was at that instant blessed beyond belief, beyond all understanding. And that state of grace had all come about purely and simply because one man and one woman – the Reverend Paul Wilson and his comfortable wife Angela, who had been perfect strangers to me until now – had decided to offer me, for one unrewarded moment, no more and no less than their kindness.

And yet of course their kindness *was* rewarded, and more handsomely than is conceivable. For neither they, nor I, will ever be able to forget it. Virtue is its own reward, I thought to myself, a reward written here for eternity on this tiny unremembered island.

Then the mood altered, as it always must, for after a few minutes two brilliant searchlights appeared low on the horizon, and they grew steadily brighter every passing second. For a moment I thought it was the comet again; but Paul jumped up. He had seen it before. 'Your plane,' he announced. 'We'd better hurry.'

My jet landed the next morning at an airbase in the Cotswolds, and I decided on a whim, having an hour or two now to spare, that on my way down to London I would stop in and see my Oxford tailor. So at about ten o'clock I was standing in the fitting room, and before he slipped the new jacket on me, he asked me to unroll my shirtsleeves. As I did so, a cascade of the purest white sand fell from the folds, onto the carpet. I apologised, but the tailor said it was no trouble, and asked, more out of politeness than serious inquiry, whether I could tell him where it had come from. Ascension Island, I said, and proceeded to tell him the story.

He listened patiently, and then, putting away his chalk and looping his tape around his neck, he said, 'You know, you are a very, very lucky man indeed. Lucky to be in such a place. Lucky to see such things. And luckiest of all to meet such very kind people. I envy you. Everyone must envy you. Wherever would you be – have you ever wondered? – without all their kindness, and without all this luck?' As he opened the door for me he put his hand briefly on my shoulder. And then I walked off into the rain.